THE CRITIC'S HORNBOOK

The Critic's Hornbook:

Reading for Interpretation

WILLIAM C. DOWLING
UNIVERSITY OF NEW MEXICO

THOMAS Y. CROWELL COMPANY
NEW YORK
Established 1834

Library of Congress Cataloging in Publication Data

Dowling, William C
    The critic's hornbook.
    Includes index.
    1. English language—Rhetoric.   2. Criticism.
3. College readers.   I. Title.
PE1479.C7D6   808'.04275   76-30884
ISBN 0-690-00884-8

Thomas Y. Crowell Company, Inc.
666 Fifth Avenue
New York, New York 10019

Manufactured in the United States of America

For L. D. Crabes

We are absurdly accustomed to the miracle of a few written signs being able to contain immortal imagery, involutions of thought, new worlds with live people, speaking, weeping, laughing. We take it for granted so simply that in a sense, by the very act of brutish routine acceptance, we undo the work of the ages. . . . What if we awake one day, all of us, and find ourselves utterly unable to read? I wish you to gasp not only at what you read but at the miracle of its being readable (so I used to tell my students).

—Vladimir Nabokov, *Pale Fire*

Contents

CONTENTS

Preface

One of the great strengths of American literary criticism in the last twenty-five or thirty years, roughly the period in which it has emerged as a coherent modern discipline, is that so much of its work has been carried forward in the classroom. If we now tend to look back on the early part of this period primarily as a time when concepts elucidated by theorists of the "new criticism" entered the mainstream, we should also recall that this was the time when teachers and students first turned their attention to the important business of close reading—the disciplined analysis of literary meaning in individual works—and when a pioneering classroom text like Brooks and Warren's *Understanding Poetry* could have an enormous impact on the teaching and learning of critical methods.

In recent years, as literary critics have come to view close analysis only as the indispensable first step toward more general interpretation, and as the emphasis in American criticism has moved ever more steadily toward a study of relations among literary works, the classroom has remained an important arena for the working out of interpretive method. In college catalogues where twenty years ago one would have found upper-level courses dealing only with major authors and periods—Shakespeare, Milton, the Age of Johnson, the Romantics— one now discovers alongside them courses organized around the concepts of theme and genre. A similar change is now widely visible even at the introductory level, where the emphasis necessarily remains both on sound literary analysis and on learning to write about literature.

As a text intended for use at this introductory level, *The Critic's*

Hornbook attempts to present and demonstrate the methods literary critics use today and to do so both systematically and in a theoretical context simplified enough to be of immediate use to the student. At the same time, I have been able to attempt a systematic and simplified presentation only because the book is intended for the classroom: though the following pages are addressed to the student, they continuously assume the presence of a teacher who looks upon the book mainly as a complement to his or her own teaching, who will want frequently either to amplify or to provide alternatives to the various points presented, and who views theory as secondary to method when literature is to be discussed in the classroom. My aim throughout the book has been to isolate and present the theoretical concepts which seem to be inseparable from method and which lead to a sensitive and intelligent reading of literary works.

Sensitive and intelligent reading is the enterprise with which *The Critic's Hornbook* is concerned, and in considering it, one may perceive the sense in which reading is the end as well as the beginning of literary study and has to do not simply with literature but with a significant dimension of human experience. The importance of the poet, Wallace Stevens said, "is that he creates the world to which we turn incessantly and without knowing it and that he gives to life the supreme fictions without which we are unable to conceive of it." Stevens used poetry as an example because he was a poet, but his notion of poetry as a body of "supreme fictions" extends to literature as a whole, to *King Lear* and *Middlemarch* as well as *Paradise Lost*, and in his phrasing we hear echoes of a view of literature that goes back through Shelley and Sir Philip Sidney to Aristotle. It is this vision of literature, not as composing a miscellaneous collection of books but as embodying a symbolic dimension of human experience without which we could not begin to conceive of the world, that seems to me to underlie the meaning and significance of modern literary study.

As the book is addressed directly to the student, I may take the occasion of the preface to say a few words to colleagues intending to use *The Critic's Hornbook* as a classroom text. These have to do with the book's presentation of critical theory and method—or, more precisely, with certain choices I was compelled to make while writing the final version.

In attempting to present systematically the methods of modern interpretation in a manner immediately accessible to the student and to isolate and briefly outline at appropriate points those theoretical principles which seem to me inseparable from method, I have sometimes found it necessary to simplify concepts which in the annals of modern criticism have a complicated history. I have, similarly, chosen to present as a coherent body of simultaneous principles a number of concepts which did not emerge simultaneously: to have ignored the influence of phenomenology and structuralism on modern interpretation, it seemed to me, would have been to exclude from a classroom text influences that are currently making their way into the classroom. I need not add that such terms as phenomenology and structuralism never appear in the text, but are simply implicit at certain points where the elements of contemporary critical method are introduced.

I may also explain that I have felt a certain obligation to bring established critical concepts into alignment with methods associated with newer approaches. As used in Chapter 4, for instance, the terms *irony* and *tension* are defined somewhat differently than when they first made their appearance, twenty or thirty years ago, in writings by theorists of the objective approach. In such cases my policy has been to retain well-established terms whenever possible—not least because they are well-established—and simply to adjust or expand their definitions to accord with contemporary methods of literary interpretation.

Finally, a word concerning the "Analysis and Interpretation" sections following Chapters 1 to 4. In these I have sought to provide the minimum amount of material for immediate classroom discussion of the interpretive methods and principles presented in those chapters and have included a series of analytic questions which may be used either as a starting point for discussion or taken by the student as an informal guide to reading outside the classroom. Chapters 5 and 6, on narrative and drama, appear without "Analysis and Interpretation" sections because those chapters have been designed to be read alongside short stories, novels, and plays chosen by the instructor as best suiting the purposes of the introductory course.

Certain of the following chapters were used, in earlier versions and mimeographed form, in courses at Harvard University and the University of New Mexico. I should like to thank my Harvard and Radcliffe students in Expository Writing 101 and my University of New Mexico students in English 294 for their reactions and suggestions and for the persistent and intelligent interrogation about critical theory and method that led me to write the book in the first place. Three deserve special thanks: Nathaniel Foote, for his kind permission to use the two versions of the critical essay which appear after Chapter 7; Mariellen Supple, whose extensive and penetrating comments on the original version of the manuscript suggested the present form of the book; and Teresa Jones, who under the pressure of press deadlines and her own heavy schedule found time to correct the final proofs.

1

READING AS ANALYSIS

Literary interpretation—the elucidation of symbolic meaning in literature—involves a logic and method that can be readily learned by anyone who has had some experience reading poems and plays and novels, but that may at first encounter seem puzzling or abstruse. To students in the first weeks of an introductory literature course, asked to analyze a poem or short story in a manner entirely new to them, and to perceive and discuss meanings they did not previously suspect to exist, the very nature of interpretation may seem to be at issue. This is a point at which one is likely to ask certain questions—why should we *analyze* literature? why can't we just read it? why do we have to discuss symbolic meaning?—that deserve answers.

One way of seeing literary interpretation in perspective is to observe that we live in a world organized by symbolic meanings, and one that demands continuous interpretation. We turn on the evening news, for instance, and hear the newscaster using such phrases as "Moscow announced today" and "the White House replied that . . ." If no such thing as symbolic meaning existed, we should have to conclude that our newscaster was talking utter nonsense—we know that Moscow is a city and the White House a building, and that cities and buildings can't make or reply to announcements, anymore than automobiles or chairs can. Yet because we are fairly expert interpreters of symbolic meaning, we understand almost without thinking about it that the newscaster is really talking about people making decisions in government.

Symbolic meaning occurs whenever we must see how one thing represents or "stands for" something else in order to comprehend it. The traffic light turns red, and we interpret its meaning when we apply our brakes. Why would we not stop for a blue light in the same situation? Because it does not represent (stand for) a command to stop. What would we say about someone who always braked when the light turned green and always drove straight through when it turned red? That he was a danger to life and limb, undoubtedly, but also that he failed to understand what red and green meant in this context, which is the same as saying that he has misunderstood their symbolic meaning.

When we come to language, we may become even more aware of a need to interpret continuously the symbolic meaning of what we hear in everyday discourse. Let us imagine the progress through the world of B, a hapless soul who does not recognize the existence of symbolic meaning:

A. He was only 58, but they put him out to pasture.

B. You mean they made him live in a *field*?

A. No, I mean they asked him to retire early. It was either that or kicking him upstairs.

B. That seems awfully cruel. Were they all going to kick him at the same time, or were they going to take turns?

A. No, I mean they were going to put him on the Board of Directors.

B. Oh. Why?

A. Because they thought he was all washed up as an executive.

B. What's wrong with that? Isn't it all right for executives to be clean?

We need not continue the dialogue to see that B is missing something here, or that his inability to interpret symbolic meaning suggests that he is going to spend the rest of his life more or less in a fog (to use an expression B wouldn't understand). When we ask exactly what it is that B is missing, we are very close to symbolic meaning as it exists in literature. Consider, for instance, A's phrase, "they put him out to pasture." The reason we say A's expression has a symbolic meaning is that it asks us to compare someone retiring from his job with a horse grown too old to draw a carriage or pull a plow—the horse is quite literally put out to pasture, and our meaning becomes symbolic only when we use the phrase to represent the condition of retired people rather than horses. When we "see what A means" by the expression, our mode of comprehension is very similar to that employed in literary interpretation.

At this point we may glimpse the answer to one of the questions with which we began: why should we discuss symbolic meaning in literature? The answer is that literature *means* symbolically, and that reading or discussing it demands a special mode of comprehension. Suppose, for instance, that someone were to ask us a simple question: "what is an aged man?" If we treat this as an ordinary request for information, we are likely to give the sort of answer that would be readily understood by our friend B: "an aged man is an elderly person of the male sex." But literature is always giving us another sort of answer, as in Yeats's poem "Sailing to Byzantium":

> An aged man is but a paltry thing,
> A tattered coat upon a stick, unless
> Soul clap its hands and sing, and louder sing
> For every tatter in its mortal dress . . . .

Something significant is being said about old age in these lines, evidently, but from the standpoint of literal meaning they just as evidently don't make any sense at all. We can imagine how someone like B would react to them: "You're trying to tell me that an aged man is a *coat*? Nonsense!" Now we are in the same position as when we overheard the earlier dialogue between A and B: we want to step into the situation and assure B that he's missing the point, that what he assumes to be nonsense makes a great deal of sense, but only when we see it in its own terms. This is what literary interpretation exists to do: we discuss symbolic meaning in these lines from Yeats because that *is* their meaning, and they are scarcely comprehensible in any other terms.

1. READING AS ANALYSIS

When we have seen that this principle lies at the very center of literary interpretation, we are in a position to answer another of the questions with which we began: why should we analyze literature? Analysis plays a double role in literary interpretation, for it both allows us to comprehend symbolic meaning and to show others why our interpretation is reasonable. When we are trying to show our friend B that expressions like "the White House announced today" and "they kicked him upstairs" possess a special kind of sense, our analysis may be brief and to the point, but this is not so even with so relatively short a poem as "Sailing to Byzantium," where a very detailed analysis is needed if we are to understand the sense of the poem.

In the next five chapters we shall be concerned with the methods of literary analysis that allow us to arrive at interpretations of poems and novels and plays. In this, our concern is with a preliminary step that makes both analysis and interpretation possible—analytic reading. The aim of analytic reading is to determine the primary or non-symbolic meaning of a text through a careful scrutiny of words and syntax, and simultaneously to note where possible symbolic meanings may occur. Since the symbolic meaning of a work is governed in a very strict sense by its primary meaning, the importance of analytic reading cannot be overstressed: any mistake at this level leads inevitably to misinterpretation at a later stage.

On the other hand, determining the primary meaning of a text, although it demands the closest attention to words and syntax, involves no techniques not used in ordinary reading, and is easily mastered with practice. What gives analytic reading its special status in criticism is that it allows us to see where symbolic meaning is likely to occur: we mark out in advance, so to speak, the areas that must be elucidated through interpretation. As the method is best demonstrated by specific questions about an actual passage, let us look at the opening lines of "Next Day," a poem by Randall Jarrell:

> Moving from Cheer to Joy, from Joy to All,
> I take a box
> And add it to my wild rice, my Cornish game hens.
> The slacked or shorted, basketed, identical
> Food-gathering flocks   5
> Are selves I overlook. Wisdom, said William James,

Is learning what to overlook. And I am wise
If that is wisdom.
Yet somehow, as I buy All from these shelves
And the boy takes it to my station wagon,   10
What I've become
Troubles me even if I shut my eyes.

When I was young and miserable and pretty
And poor, I'd wish
What all girls wish: to have a husband,   15
A house and children. Now that I'm old, my wish
Is womanish:
That the boy putting groceries in my car

See me. It bewilders me he doesn't see me.

Now let us see how an emphasis on primary meaning allows us to
isolate possibilities of symbolic meaning:

Line 1: What is *Cheer*? *Joy*? *All*?
Line 3: What is *wild rice*? What are *Cornish game hens*?
Line 4: What does *slacked* mean? *shorted*?
Line 5: What are *food-gathering flocks*?
Line 6: What does *selves* mean? Who is *William James*?
Line 10: To what does *it* refer?
Line 19: What does *see* mean?

Since we live in twentieth-century America, we are likely to have
little trouble with *Cheer* and *Joy* and *All*—they are the brand names
of detergents, and this primary meaning immediately suggests that
our speaker is someone shopping in a supermarket. Are there any
possibilities of symbolic meaning here? Suppose we take away the
capital letters from *Cheer* and *Joy*, getting two words normally used
to describe not detergents but emotions (as in "she was cheerful"
or "she was joyful"). And *All* as it stands in line 1 suggests a standard
philosophical abstraction: "the totality of what there is." Does anything later in the passage suggest that these meanings may also be
relevant to what the speaker is saying?

When we consider their primary meaning, neither *wild rice* nor
Cornish game hens seem to present any problem: wild rice is simply
rice that grows in the wild (as distinct from rice cultivated by people
for their own use), and Cornish game hens are a kind of domestic

5

fowl bred to resemble the game birds that, in earlier centuries, people used to hunt for food. Are there, then, any suggestions of symbolic meaning here? One possibility seems to lie in something wild rice and Cornish game hens have in common: sitting on the shelves of a supermarket, surrounded by modern products like Cheer and Joy and All, they remind us of a time when people hunted and gathered their food in the wild. Is this relevant to understanding what the speaker is saying?

We may have to pause a moment before we see that *slacked* must mean "wearing slacks," *shorted* must mean "wearing shorts," and *basketed* must (since this is a supermarket) mean "carrying or pushing a basket." Here it is the syntax that is likely to draw our attention, for to describe suburban housewives shopping in a supermarket as *slacked or shorted, basketed* is to give equal status to the features that make them seem *identical* (exactly like each other) to the speaker. The oddness of using *basketed* to mean "carrying or pushing a basket" is thus explained through the syntactic parallel with *slacked* and *shorted*: it reveals what for the speaker is the oddness of the scene being described.

When we come to *food-gathering flocks*, we immediately recognize that we are in the area of symbolic meaning, for on the level of primary meaning the phrase has to do not with housewives shopping in supermarkets but with creatures gathering food in some natural habitat. (How is this supported by what we said above about the possible symbolic implication of *wild rice* and *Cornish game hens*?) We are already making a kind of statement about symbolic meaning, therefore, when we say "by *food-gathering flocks* the speaker means housewives shopping in a supermarket," or (a more precise formulation) "in line 5 the speaker describes housewives shopping in a supermarket as *food-gathering flocks*."

How do we know that the speaker is describing housewives? Here we may see exactly how an emphasis on primary meaning allows us to isolate symbolic meaning. It might occur to us to give a general answer: "the speaker is herself a housewife shopping in a supermarket, and she strongly implies that she is describing other women just like her." But suppose someone were to ask how we know that the speaker is a housewife shopping in a supermarket? Now our answer will focus on the primary meaning of such words and phrases as *Cheer,*

Joy, All, wild rice, Cornish game hens, the boy putting groceries in my car, etc., showing how these elements determine our sense of the scene as a whole.

When we come to *selves* in line 6, we may have to pause a moment to see that we are dealing with another instance of symbolic meaning. For although it may be obvious that what the speaker *means* is something like "these women are so much like me that they seem like versions of me" (and we could introduce this meaning as evidence that both the speaker and the women she is describing are housewives in a supermarket), what the speaker is *saying* is "these women are me." Like any similar expression—e.g., "I am you," "John is Harry"—this can have meaning only on the symbolic level.

We may have to do a bit of outside research before we discover that *William James* is a philosopher, but the discovery immediately suggests something significant both about the speaker and the possible symbolic meaning of an earlier line. When we were discussing the meaning of *All* in line 1, we may recall, we noted that besides being the brand name of a detergent it was an abstraction common in philosophy: "the totality of what there is." Now we discover that our speaker is not merely a housewife, but a housewife familiar enough with modern philosophy that an ordinary scene in a supermarket reminds her of a phrase from William James. How does this strengthen our sense that *All* has a possible symbolic meaning?

If we keep this question in mind, we shall see the importance of *it* in line 10, the antecedent of which is *All* in the preceding line. Here the syntax gives us the primary meaning of the line: "I buy detergent from these supermarket shelves, and the boy takes it, along with my other groceries, out to my station wagon." Yet the speaker doesn't say "along with my other groceries": she says "I buy All from these shelves / And the boy takes *it* to my station wagon." Given what we know about the possible symbolic meaning of *All*, what might this mean in symbolic terms?

Finally, we come in line 19 to another instance of what seems to be symbolic meaning: we know that the primary meaning of *see* is "to perceive visually," and it is clear that the boy who works in this supermarket sees well enough to pack groceries, take them out into the parking lot, load them into station wagons, etc. To understand what the speaker means, then, we must evidently comprehend something other than the primary meaning of *see*—compare, for instance, the symbolic sense of such expressions as "he looked right through me"—and this leads us to a consideration of symbolic meaning.

An analytic reading of these lines, then, allows us both to determine primary meaning and to see in very precise terms where the possibilities of symbolic meaning lie. Once we have done so, it might seem as though we could immediately begin to explain the symbolic meaning of such words and phrases as *Joy* and *All* and *food-gathering flocks*, but for several reasons this is not the case: although we might manage to make some perceptive comments about the symbolic meaning of such words and phrases without further analysis, we should soon find that, not being controlled by a sense of symbolic meaning in the passage as a whole, they were random and disconnected.

When our explanation *is* controlled by a sense of symbolic meaning in the passage as a whole, on the other hand, we shall be able not only to explain the symbolic meaning of these isolated words and phrases but to show how they relate to each other within the total context of the poem. To achieve this we must defer interpretation for the moment and turn to the first of the several stages of literary analysis that precede interpretation. This our analytic reading will have prepared us to do.

Neither the words nor the syntax of a contemporary work like Jarrell's poem "Next Day" is likely to present us with any particular problem: the speaker's world, like our own, is twentieth-century America, and she speaks an idiom very close to ours. Yet even an introductory study of literature will soon convey us into worlds very different from our own—in the world of Victorian fiction, for instance, or of Shakespeare's plays, we shall find neither supermarkets nor station wagons—and where men and women speak in idioms somewhat different from our own.

Yet it remains true that analytic reading provides our means of entry into the world of any literary work, whether it is a contemporary poem or an Elizabethan play, so a few words must be said in this chapter about the special problems involved in reading the poetry and prose of earlier periods. Let us consider, first of all, the problem of language: since one of the objects of analytic reading is to penetrate the idiom of some speaker or narrator, and since the idioms of literary English have changed along with the English language, a modern reader needs considerable literary experience before the poetry and prose of, say, the sixteenth or seventeenth centuries becomes as accessible as that of our own time.

Suppose, for instance, that we were to read our way backwards through any standard anthology of English literature, beginning with the contemporary selections and reading back toward the poetry and prose of the Middle Ages. By the time we arrived at the early seventeenth century, the period of Shakespeare's later plays, we would notice that the language had long since lost its modern look, and that we were glancing almost automatically at the footnotes that give the meanings of words no longer used in modern English, or that explain the intricacies of a syntax more elaborate than our own. Yet even at this point we would be reading a version of English comprehensible (with footnotes) in modern terms, so let us continue our experiment and go back yet another 200 years, to the very beginning of English in its modern form. Here is Chaucer's Wife of Bath, who is, like the speaker of Jarrell's "Next Day," a housewife, explaining to the company of pilgrims in *The Canterbury Tales* that she has outlived five husbands and is presently looking for a sixth:

> Blessed be God that I have wedded five,
> Of whiche I have piked out the beste,
> Bothe of hir nether purs and of hir cheste.
> Diverse scoles maken parfit clerkes,
> And diverse practikes in sondry werkes
> Maken the werkman parfit sikerly:
> Of five housbondes scoleying am I.
> Welcome the sixte whan that evere he shal!

The Wife of Bath is one of the great comic characters in English literature, but it is evident that to enjoy the comedy we must learn to read a version of English barely recognizable in modern terms. Or is it so unrecognizable? Let us look, for instance, at the first three lines, which suggest that the Wife's five husbands, having had the fortune (or misfortune) to marry a woman of formidable sexual appetite, have died not through mishap or old age but of sheer sexual exhaustion. The first line can be read by any reader of modern

English: *blessed be God that I have wedded five* means "I bless God that I have married (had the good fortune to marry) five men." The next line, however, although its meaning depends on a sense of *pick* related both to one modern use of the word—"I got to the sale early and picked out the best dress"—and to an earlier sense that survives in the word *pickpocket*, is less comprehensible to the modern ear: "five husbands," the Wife is saying, "from whom I have taken the best (most valuable) they had."

What is the Wife saying she has taken from her husbands? When we know that *hir* is an older form of *their*, and that *cheste* means *money chest* or *strongbox*, we may realize that part of what the Wife is saying in the third line is that she has grown wealthy through inheriting the fortunes of five successive husbands. Yet that is only part of her meaning, and even when we discover that *purs* means, as in modern English, *purse*, and that *nether* means *lower* or *below*, we still find ourselves confronted with an instance of symbolic meaning—the *nether purs* is, metaphorically, the sac that contains the testicles, and the Wife is boasting indirectly about having emptied this "purse" of the semen expended in her husbands' sexual climaxes. When we begin to ask why the Wife describes the sexual exhaustion of her five husbands in terms symbolically related to money and other valuables, we are in the same area of analytic reading as when we isolated the possibilities of symbolic meaning contained in *Cheer* and *Joy* and *All* in line 1 of "Next Day."

Our exercise, it goes without saying, has carried us far beyond the concerns of any introductory literature course—traveling the road to Canterbury with the Wife of Bath and her fellow pilgrims is one of the great rewards of advanced literary study—but our example may illustrate the manner in which analytic reading becomes progressively more demanding as we move into the poetry and prose of earlier centuries. Yet it is also true—and this is the point to be stressed here—that this poetry and prose invariably looks more difficult than it really is to readers whose only experience has been with contemporary literature, and one of the early rewards of introductory literary study is discovering that, with some practice and a good deal of concentration, English literature as far back as Shakespeare may be read with the same comprehension and enjoyment as modern literature.

To see why this is so, let us examine the first stanza of John Donne's "Love's Alchemy," a poem written in the early seventeenth century. As in our reading of the opening lines of "Next Day," our object is to determine primary meaning while isolating possible areas of symbolic meaning. Now, however, determining primary meaning will involve looking up some words and phrases that have passed out of common usage, and dealing with syntax that may in some cases seem unfamiliar:

> Some that have deeper digged love's mine than I,
> Say where his centric happiness doth lie;
>   I have loved, and got, and told,
> But should I love, get, tell, till I were old,
> I should not find that hidden mystery;   5
>   O, 'tis imposture all:
> And as no chemic yet the elixir got,
>   But glorifies his pregnant pot,
>   If by the way to him befall
> Some odoriferous thing, or medicinal;   10
>   So lovers dream a rich and long delight,
>   But get a winter-seeming summer's night.

Now, as with our earlier example, let us consider some specific questions:

Title: What is *alchemy*?
Line 1: To whom does *some* refer?
Line 2: What does *say* mean? *centric*? To whom does *his* refer?
Line 3: What does *got* mean? *told*?
Line 5: What is *that hidden mystery*?
Line 7: What does *as* mean? *chemic*? *elixir*?
Line 8: What does *but* mean? *glorifies*? *pregnant*? *pot*?
Line 9: Explain the phrase *if by the way to him befall*.
Line 10: What does *odoriferous* mean?
Line 11: What does *so* mean? *dream*?
Line 12: Explain *winter-seeming summer's night*.

To answer these questions is to put ourselves in the world of the speaker, just as we earlier put ourselves in the world of the suburban housewife who speaks in "Next Day." In determining the primary

meaning of these lines, let us use the method of explicative paraphrase, which is often used in the analytic reading of prose and poetry
written in earlier periods.

Title: *alchemy* was the medieval pseudoscience that sought to
devise a method for turning base metals into gold. But nobody ever
discovered the secret, and that's one important thing about Donne's
title: he's comparing the futility of the alchemist's search for gold
to the futility of the lover's search for fulfillment in love. (Another
important thing is that alchemy was sometimes used to defraud
innocent people. See line 6: *O, 'tis imposture all.*)

Line 1: *some* means "somebody," as in the sentence, "Somebody
tell me how to get there."

Line 2: *say* means "tell," as in "tell me, please." *centric* means
"in or at the center." *his* means "love's."

Now we might try a paraphrase of the first sentence. The sentence
means something like "Somebody who has more experience in these
matters than I have, please tell me how you're supposed to go about
attaining happiness in love." But we notice that Donne's metaphor,
which uses the phrase *digged deeper in love's mine* to say "had more
experience in love," is comparing the lover's search for happiness to a
search for hidden gold.

Line 3: *got*, means, of course, "acquired," but in a sense that
associates it with wealth (gold). *told* means "counted."

Line 5: *that hidden mystery* is *where his centric happiness doth
lie.*

Now let's try a paraphrase of lines 3–5. The lines mean something
like "I have loved women, and slept with them, and calculated the
happiness I got from sleeping with them, and I have the feeling that
if I did the same thing from now until I was an old man, I'd still never
discover why people keep describing sexual love as a mystical experience."

How, you might be asking yourself, did we get from the simple
line *I have loved, and got, and told* to all this about sex? The process
of inference illustrates what close reading is all about. First, the word
love is used by a male speaker, and must refer to love of women, and
it is obvious from the context that he sees women as objects to possess:
I have loved means "I have been emotionally attracted to certain
women and desired to possess them." There are perhaps any number

of ways for a man to possess a woman, but the most obvious way is sexually. Our expectation that this is what the poet means here is fulfilled when he uses two words usually associated with the possession of money (*got* and *told*) to describe his relations with women. The metaphor is a reflection of the speaker's attitude toward women, and in using it he reveals that he has been keeping track of his love affairs in the same spirit as some men keep track of their money. The whole idea suggests sexual love (possession of a woman's body) as the thing being talked about.

Line 7: *as* means "just as." *chemic* means "alchemist." The *elixir* is the substance that alchemists thought would turn base metals into gold (if they could discover what it was).

Line 8: *but* means "but he." *glorifies* means "praises." *pregnant* means "fruitful" or "productive." *pot* is the vessel in which the alchemist is trying to mix up the elixir.

Line 9: *if by the way to him befall* means "if the alchemist, while he is trying to mix up the elixir, happens by chance to produce . . ."

Line 10: *odoriferous* probably suggests to you something that smells bad, as in "those socks are pretty odoriferous." But here it means "sweet-smelling" or "pleasantly scented." How do we know? Because (1) *odoriferous* is paired with *medicinal,* which means "useful as medicine," and the parallelism suggests that it, too, refers to something good, and (2) the alchemist seems pretty pleased about producing something *odoriferous,* which he wouldn't if it smelled bad.

Line 11: *so* means "in the same way." *dream* means "dream about" or (more literally) "imagine that they are going to have."

Line 12: *winter-seeming summer's night* means "an experience that, though it was supposed to be like a long and pleasant night in summer, turns out to be more like a short and freezing night in the middle of winter."

Since we've gone over the words and phrases in lines 7–12, we might try writing out a paraphrase of those lines.

Lines 7–12 mean something like this: "even though no alchemist ever discovered the magic elixir that turns metals to gold, you always hear alchemists boasting about some minor thing they've discovered by chance; in the same way, people fall in love expecting to find some magic happiness, and all they really find is some minor pleasure." Again, the comparison suggests that this minor pleasure is sex, and

13

that when lovers talk about sex being a mystical experience, they're acting like the alchemist who settles for a new perfume or headache remedy when he was really after the famous elixir.

No beginning reader who had wrong answers, or no answers, to the questions above should feel bad—Donne is a difficult poet, and a reader has to work pretty hard to figure out his meaning. Anyone who *can* figure out a Donne poem, however, is prepared to read any English writer from Shakespeare to W. H. Auden with perfect critical understanding. So let's see how literary critics go about reading passages like this one.

There are, we've said, two major problems in any passage: words and syntax. The syntax in this example is relatively uncomplicated, but there are a couple of places where we have to pay close attention to understand what's going on. Consider, for instance, the word *his* in line 2: if we are aware that writers in Donne's time often used *his* where we'd now use *its,* we can figure out immediately that *his* goes with *love's* in line 1, and that the phrase *his centric happiness* means *love's centric happiness.* But a simpler way is just to watch the syntax: lines 1–2 together form a complete sentence, and the only thing in the sentence with which *his* can possibly go is *love.*

The trick, with both *his* and *that hidden mystery,* is to go back and look for the proper antecedent. "Proper antecedent" may sound like a phrase from a high school grammar book, but it's simply meant to suggest that words like *his* and *that* should immediately bring a question to mind—*his centric happiness* (whose centric happiness?), *that hidden mystery* (what hidden mystery?)—and that figuring out the syntax of a passage means answering a series of such questions.

Another kind of problem is represented by *as no chemic yet the elixir got,* in line 7. We've already observed that *as* means "just as" (that's something we can figure out by reading the line carefully), and once we know that we should immediately ask ourselves what phrase is going to complete the sentence. In this case, it's not a missing antecedent that bothers us, but a feeling of expectation that comes when we see that single word *as* standing all alone.

Let's look at a more obvious example: if George and I are talking, and George begins a sentence by saying "Just as Americans drink milk with their meals . . .", I feel cheated unless there's another part to the sentence ("... the French drink wine with theirs"). That is, my awareness of the requirements of English syntax tells me that nobody goes around saying things like "Just as Americans drink milk with their meals" (period).

When we come to the word *as* in line 7, then, we have the same feeling of expectation, and we aren't satisfied until we come across the phrase that completes the thought; in this case, it's way down in line 11: *so lovers dream a rich and long delight.* Once we have made the *as/so* connection, we're on our way to figuring out Donne's comparison—"just as alchemists do this, lovers do that"—and to a complete understanding of the sentence.

Finally, let's look at the word *dream* in line 11. As it stands, it looks like the phrase *lovers dream* might be complete in itself (lovers dream, dogs bark, children play). But then we read the entire line— *lovers dream a rich and long delight*—and we realize that we've got to account for *a rich and long delight.* To make sense of the sentence, we have to supply a word; otherwise the line is roughly equivalent to "I dream airplanes every night." The word is, of course, "about" —"lovers dream about a rich and long delight," "I dream about airplanes every night." Writers, and especially poets, are always leaving words out of sentences this way, and putting them back in is something we must do to understand the syntax.

In reading literature closely, of course, we shall often come across problems in syntax more complicated than these, but the process of solving them is always the same: whenever you strike a sentence that doesn't make perfect sense, you isolate the crucial word or phrase and figure out its function, then go back and reconstruct the sentence in a way that does make sense. After a while one learns to recognize the vague feeling of uneasiness that comes when one hasn't understood the precise relation of every word in a passage to every other word, and untangling the syntax becomes an automatic process.

Even if the syntax of our passage didn't give you any trouble, the words probably did. Because Donne wrote his poetry over three centuries ago, and the English language has changed a good deal since, a big part of reading "Love's Alchemy" consists of recovering the meaning of words and phrases we no longer use, or that are used in senses that have grown unfamiliar.

15

1. READING AS ANALYSIS

Most professors nowadays teach from paperback college editions designed to help solve this problem, both by changing the spelling and punctuation of older texts to conform with modern practice ("normalizing") and by supplying the meanings of difficult words and phrases in the margin or at the bottom of the page ("glossing"). The idea behind these editions—to make earlier literature accessible to modern readers—is splendid, but they vary widely in quality, and one has to use them carefully.

Carefully means, in this case, sceptically. Unfortunately, many editors of college editions are occasionally lazy (they neglect to gloss important words), or oblivious (they don't realize that words familiar to them may be strange to you), or simply incompetent (they misread a line, and give you a gloss that supplies the wrong meaning for the context). So if you strike a word that isn't glossed at the bottom of the page, or a gloss that seems mistaken, you may have to check it yourself.

I took the first stanza of "Love's Alchemy," for instance, from the paperback edition of Donne that I used as an undergraduate, one that is reasonably well edited and usually dependable. But although the editor glosses, in the first twelve lines, *chemic, elixir,* and *pregnant,* he gives no meanings for *centric, got, told,* etc. How, then, do we find out what those words mean?

The secret is a magnificent twelve-volume work entitled *The Oxford English Dictionary,* to which scholars and critics always refer as the *OED,* and which is in the reference room of every college library. The importance of the *OED* for the literary critic can't be overestimated: I sometimes think that two-thirds of close reading is simply learning about the existence of the *OED,* and the other third is learning how to use it.

Of all the words in the Donne passage that our editor didn't gloss, *got* and *told* seem to be the most crucial, not only because Donne is using each in a sense that is no longer current, but because both words have modern meanings ("George got an A on the exam and told his roommate about it") that, if we're not careful, could easily mislead us. Suppose, however, that we've been attentive enough to realize that these modern meanings don't fit the passage (Donne doesn't say what he *got,* and he doesn't seem to have *told* anything to anyone), and we have to find the ones that do.

At this point, we add *got* and *told* to our list of unglossed words (*centric* was an obvious choice: nobody uses it anymore) and head for the library. With the *OED* open in front of us, we begin to search for a meaning of *got* that fits the passage. The *OED*, we discover, contains not only definitions of words, but examples of their use, and the dates of the works from which the examples were taken. So we have three questions to answer: (1) which definition of *got* is appropriate to Donne's meaning; (2) do the examples in the *OED* use the word in a similar sense; and (3) was that sense current usage when Donne wrote "Love's Alchemy"?

The *OED* has several pages of definitions for *get*, but only one seems appropriate here: "to acquire wealth or property"—that would explain why Donne didn't feel it necessary to tell us what he got: "wealth or property" is understood as part of the meaning. When we look at examples for this definition, our guess is confirmed. There are a number of examples; let's look at just one:

> 1677 Evelyn, *Diary* 10 Sept: Whilst he was Secretary of State
> . . . he had gotten vastly, but spent it as hastily.

1677 is, of course, the date of this particular occurrence of this form of *get*; there are earlier examples, and we discover that the usage was current when Donne wrote. "Evelyn, *Diary* 10 Sept" is an abbreviated reference to the source of the quote. But the important thing is the example itself: Evelyn is using *get* in the same sense Donne did, and this is our final assurance that the definition is the one we want.

When we've discovered what *got* means, *told* is easy. Again, the *OED* gives lots of definitions, but the one that's most likely to catch our eye at this point is "to reckon up or calculate the total amount or value of (money or other things); to count." This is a meaning of *told* that survives now in the phrase "untold wealth" ("so much wealth it can't all be counted"), and we choose it immediately because it so obviously complements the meaning we just settled on for *got*.

Now we are ready to proceed to a reading of the line, and to arrive at the extended meaning we've already discussed briefly: since both *got* and *told* are words associated with the possession of property, and since the speaker in "Love's Alchemy" is using them to describe his love affairs, we are justified in viewing him as a man who sees women as objects to possess. This is a metaphoric meaning, the sort of thing we'll be discussing in later chapters (and the sort of thing one writes papers about), but it all starts with the unexciting business of

1. READING AS ANALYSIS

discovering exactly what words mean, of putting in our time with the text of "Love's Alchemy" and the *OED*.

It is often said that you must be a good scholar before you can be a good critic, and the process we went through to discover the meaning of the line *I have loved, and got, and told* is a perfect illustration of the point. Our detective work with the *OED* isn't simply a matter of looking up words in a dictionary, it's a form of philological research, of recovering meanings that are moribund now, but that are alive and full of implication in Donne's poems and Shakespeare's plays. This process of recovery is what scholarship, on all its levels, is about.

With later literature, of course, this sort of problem doesn't come up as often: reading *The Sun Also Rises* demands less time and intellectual energy than reading *Hamlet*, simply because Hemingway is writing a language more familiar to us than Shakespeare's. Yet it is only a matter of time before readers of Randall Jarrell will have to look up such terms as *Cheer* and *Joy*, just as we look up the meaning of words in Shakespeare and Milton. All this is simply part of learning how to read literature in any period: the amount of time one puts in figuring out a passage of Donne pays huge dividends, and it does not take long before one leaves the *OED* behind and reads Donne's poetry as comfortably as that of any contemporary poet.

ANALYSIS AND INTERPRETATION

The selections below, like those in the "Analysis and Interpretation" sections following Chapters 2 through 4, are provided to allow practice in connection with the critical techniques or concepts discussed in the chapter immediately preceding. In this section our concern is with analytic reading, and our strategy in each case is the same as we adopted in the case of Jarrell's "Next Day" and Donne's "Love's Alchemy." Answers to questions about the meaning of words and phrases should be checked against the appropriate entry in the *OED*. Explanations of syntax should take the form of a correct paraphrase.

THOMAS HARDY

NEW YEAR'S EVE

"I have finished another year," said God,
   "In grey, green, white, and brown;

I have strewn the leaf upon the sod,
Sealed up the worm within the clod,
 And let the last sun down."   5

"And what's the good of it?" I said,
 "What reasons made you call
From formless void this earth we tread,
When nine-and-ninety can be read
 Why nought should be at all?   10

"Yea, Sire; why shaped you us, 'who in
 This tabernacle groan'—
If ever a joy be found herein,
Such joy no man had wished to win
 If he had never known!"   15

Then he: "My labours—logicless—
 You may explain; not I:
Sense-sealed I have wrought, without a guess
That I evolved a Consciousness
 To ask for reasons why.   20

"Strange that ephemeral creatures who
 By my own ordering are,
Should see the shortness of my view,
Use ethic tests I never knew,
 Or made provision for!"   25

He sank to raptness as of yore,
 And opening New Year's Day
Wove it by rote as theretofore,
And went on working evermore
 In his unweeting way.   30

What are the appropriate meanings of *clod, nought, tabernacle, logicless, sense-sealed, ephemeral, raptness, unweeting?*

What is the syntactic explanation of *can be read* (9), *why shaped you us* (11), *no man had wished to win* (14), *sense-sealed I have wrought* (18), *by my own ordering* (22), *sank to raptness* (26), *as theretofore* (28)?

GERARD MANLEY HOPKINS

DUNS SCOTUS'S OXFORD

Towery city and branchy between towers;
Cuckoo-echoing, bell-swarmèd, lark-charmèd, rook-racked,
 river-rounded;

> The dapple-eared lily below thee; that country and town did
> Once encounter in, here coped and poisèd powers;
>
> Thou hast a base and brickish skirt there, sours   5
> That neighbour-nature thy grey beauty is grounded
> Best in; graceless growth, thou hast confounded
> Rural rural keeping—folk, flocks, and flowers.
>
> Yet ah! this air I gather and I release
> He lived on; these weeds and waters, these walls are what   10
> He haunted who of all men most sways my spirits to peace;
>
> Of realty the rarest-veinèd unraveller; a not
> Rivalled insight, be rival Italy or Greece;
> Who fired France for Mary without spot.

What are the appropriate meanings of *towery, branchy, bell-swarmèd, rook-racked, coped, brickish, confounded, realty, spot?*

What is the syntactic explanation of *once encounter in* (4), *sours / That neighbour-nature* (5–6), *thou hast confounded rural rural keeping* (7–8), *be rival Italy or Greece* (13), *who fired France* (14)?

Who is *he* in line 10?

Who is Duns Scotus? (How do we find out?)

RICHARD HOOKER

From *OF THE LAWS OF ECCLESIASTICAL POLITY*

Now if Nature should intermit her course and leave altogether, though it were but for a while, the observation of her own laws; if those principle and mother elements of the world, whereof all things in this lower world are made, should lose the qualities which they now have; if the frame of that heavenly arch erected over our   5 heads should loosen and dissolve itself; if celestial spheres should forget their wonted motions and by irregular volubility turn themselves any way as it might happen; if the prince of the lights of heaven which now as a giant doth run his unwearied course, should as it were through a languishing faintness begin to stand and to   10 rest himself; if the moon should wander from her beaten way, the times and seasons of the year blend themselves by disordered and confused mixture, the winds breathe out their last gasp, the clouds yield no rain, the earth be defeated of heavenly influence, the fruits of the earth pine away as children at the withered breasts of their   15 mother no longer able to yield them relief, what would become of man himself, whom these things now do all serve? See we not

plainly that obedience of creatures unto the law of Nature is the
stay of the whole world?

What are the appropriate meanings of *intermit, observation, frame,
wonted, volubility, stand, beaten, defeated, stay?*

What are the syntactic explanations of *leave altogether* (1),
whereof (3), *which* (9) *his* (9), *begin to stand* (10), *by disordered
and confused mixture* (12–13), *be defeated of* (14), *yield them relief*
(16)?

As a final exercise for this chapter, you might construct a "reading
edition" of one of the previous poems or passages—that is, supply the
footnotes that would appear in a well-edited anthology for the modern
reader. When glossing difficult words or phrases, it is not necessary to
quote the *OED* exactly: you may supply a simplified definition appropriate to the context. When supplying an explanatory footnote for
syntactically difficult lines or passages, provide a paraphrase that clari-
fies the meaning.

How does your "edition" of the poem or passage compare with
those available in published anthologies? Do any of the footnotes sup-
plied by other editors strike you as being mistaken or inadequate? In
case of disagreement, how would you defend the superiority of your
reading?

2

SPEAKER AND AUDIENCE

One way of viewing literature is as a kind of direct communication—that is, an author has a message to get across, or a story to tell, and in doing so speaks directly to his or her readers. When Keats, for instance, begins a sonnet with these words—

> When I have fears that I may cease to be
> Before my pen has gleaned my teeming brain, . . .

—and then goes on to describe the thoughts he has when he contemplates his own early death, we know immediately who is speaking: John Keats (1795–1821), a Romantic poet who died of consumption at the early age of 25.

This seems like a plausible enough theory of how a literary work communicates its meaning, and for a long time it was the accepted one. But then it was pointed out that the theory presented certain difficulties. What are we to do, for instance, with situations in which the "I" of a poem or a story cannot be identified with the author? Consider these lines from a poem by Robert Browning:

> I am grown peaceful as old age tonight.
> I regret little, I would change still less.
> Since there my past life lies, why alter it?

These lines are spoken by Andrea del Sarto, an artist who lived in Florence around the turn of the fifteenth century, and whose story Browning read about in Vasari's *Lives of the Painters*. "Andrea del Sarto" is a dramatic monologue—a kind of poem in which an imaginary speaker addresses a listener in his presence, and in the course of his speech reveals something about himself and his situation (in this case, we discover that Andrea is a highly gifted painter who, because of certain moral failings, will never become really great). If the Renaissance painter Andrea del Sarto had actually written this poem, there would be no problem: his monologue would be just like Keats's sonnet, a direct expression of his personal thoughts. But because the poem was written by Robert Browning, an English poet who lived some three centuries after the real Andrea, we are forced to make a distinction between author and speaker.

There are many literary works that ask us to make this distinction between author and speaker, and in obvious cases we do so almost without thinking about it. When we read *Huckleberry Finn*, for instance, we realize immediately that the story is being told by a half-educated teenage boy who runs away and floats down the Mississippi River on a raft, and not by Mark Twain, the white-haired author and lecturer. The same is true, in fact, of any first-person novel, of satires like *Gulliver's Travels* (where we never confuse Lemuel Gulliver, the somewhat witless ship's surgeon who tells the story, with the author Jonathan Swift), and of any number of poems that, like "Andrea del Sarto," have imaginary speakers.

To deal with this situation, literary critics adopted the term "persona" to describe an imaginary speaker who could not be identified with the author; thus, one referred to Gulliver as Jonathan Swift's "satiric persona." This seemed to settle the matter nicely, by splitting literature up into two categories: works like Keats's sonnet, in which speaker and author were the same, and works like "Andrea del Sarto," in which they were different.

At this point, however, another group of critics made an important distinction. "The imaginary speaker to whom you refer as a 'persona,'" they pointed out to their colleagues, "is someone who exists *inside* the work, and the author is someone who exists *outside* it. When we read *Huckleberry Finn*, after all, we discover that the whole story is told by Huck: Mark Twain never says a word. So why bother calling Huck 'Mark Twain's persona'? Why not just call him the narrator?"

This has become one of the central principles of modern literary criticism, and it is one that demands careful consideration. To say that the speaker of a poem or the narrator of a story exists inside the work means not only that he is a different person than the author, but that he belongs to a different sphere of reality than the author. Authors, like the rest of us, are flesh-and-blood beings who live and die, and imaginary speakers never do: Robert Browning has been buried in Westminster Abbey for almost a hundred years, but Andrea del Sarto is exactly the same age today as he was in 1855, when he first appeared in the world, and we hear his voice now exactly as readers did then.

At this point, another question suggests itself: it is logical to distinguish between author and speaker in "Andrea del Sarto" and *Huckleberry Finn*, so isn't it also logical to distinguish between the real John Keats (who is buried in the Protestant Cemetery in Rome) and the young speaker who contemplates his own death in "When I Have Fears"? The answer, of course, is yes: every poem and novel and essay has a speaker who exists only inside the work. The distinction between the actual Keats and the young poet whose voice we hear in the sonnet may seem less obvious than the one between Browning and Andrea del Sarto, but in principle it is exactly the same.

The terms *speaker* and *narrator* both refer to the imaginary being who speaks to us from the pages of a literary work. In practice, "speaker" is normally used when we are discussing a short work (a sonnet, an essay, a lyric poem), "narrator" when we are discussing a longer work that contains a story.

Once we focus on the concept of the fictional speaker, we are ready to begin critical analysis. Everything we can discover about the speaker will help us to a more complete interpretation of the work we are reading. Usually it is best to start with things like sex and age and occupation, not only because these are readily identified but because they determine the way the speaker views the world. It is extremely important, for instance, that the narrator of *Tom Jones* is a man and the narrator of *Pride and Prejudice* a woman, that the speaker in George Herbert's "The Collar" is a clergyman and that Browning's Andrea del Sarto is a painter, that Holden Caulfield, in J. D. Salinger's *The Catcher in the Rye*, is a teenager and that the speaker in T. S. Eliot's "Gerontion" is an old man.

Our method of analysis, which uses everything we have learned from our previous analytic reading of the work, once again focuses not on symbolic meaning but on possibilities of symbolic meaning. Since we know in a general sense what those possibilities are, we now undertake to analyze in detail the dramatic context in which symbolic meaning occurs. Our analysis of speaker or narrator is the first step in this process, one that will later allow us to show in very precise terms how the symbolic meaning of the work derives from the way the speaker views not only the world but his or her own situation in the world.

At the same time, analysis of speaker or narrator allows us to reformulate in more specific terms what we earlier saw as possibilities of symbolic meaning in the work: although we are still not prepared to make any conclusive statements about symbolic meaning, we are eliminating certain possibilities and confirming others as we proceed. To see in more detail how we undertake this stage of critical analysis, let us again look at the opening lines of Jarrell's "Next Day":

> Moving from Cheer to Joy, from Joy to All,
> I take a box
> And add it to my wild rice, my Cornish game hens.
> The slacked or shorted, basketed, identical
> Food-gathering flocks   5
> Are selves I overlook. Wisdom, said William James,
>
> Is learning what to overlook. And I am wise
> If that is wisdom.
> Yet somehow, as I buy All from these shelves
> And the boy takes it to my station wagon,   10
> What I've become
> Troubles me even if I shut my eyes.

When I was young and miserable and pretty
And poor, I'd wish
What all girls wish: to have a husband,   15
A house and children. Now that I'm old, my wish
Is womanish:
That the boy putting groceries in my car

See me. It bewilders me he doesn't see me.

When we earlier undertook an analytic reading of these lines, our questions were about the meaning of specific words and phrases; now we are ready to focus on the speaker. How do we know, for instance, that the speaker is a woman? The answer in this case may seem obvious, for the speaker says *when I was young . . . I'd wish | What all girls wish*—since anyone who was a girl grows up to be a woman, the speaker must be a woman.

Notice, however, that the occurrence of the word *pretty* in line 13 by itself contains a strong suggestion that the speaker is female. If we were given only lines 1–13 of the poem to analyze, we should still be inclined to say that the speaker is a woman, since a male speaker in this situation would be likely to describe himself as handsome rather than pretty. In many works, we must determine something as central as the speaker's sex through just such indirect suggestions.

Although it might seem equally obvious that our speaker is not only a woman but a housewife, our analysis assumes the responsibility of showing why this must be so. We again look, therefore, to what the speaker says about herself: *I'd wish | What all girls wish: to have a husband, | A house and children.* Our sense that her wish has been fulfilled is now confirmed by all the other details which suggest a housewife shopping in a supermarket: *groceries, station wagon,* etc.

Suppose, however, that someone were to ask us how we knew that the speaker was in a supermarket, and not in a bank or an airport? Our answer would of course introduce all the details that suggest a supermarket rather than any other setting: *Cheer, Joy,* and *All,* we would point out, aren't sold in banks or airports (notice how this focuses on the *primary* meaning of *Cheer, Joy,* and *All*); neither do banks and airports have baskets (here we point to *basketed*) or *shelves,* boys to carry *groceries* to the *cars* of customers, etc.

Only someone very determined to ignore the obvious, we might guess, could resist the force of our argument. Yet our argument in fact takes account of a very complex phenomenon, for it is not as though we had any real supermarket to point to in this situation: the various elements we introduce as evidence *define* the idea of "supermarket" in these lines—it is, in a manner of speaking, a supermarket created out of the very elements to which we point in our argument. Our analysis of speaker and situation, therefore, is really an analysis of the way in which the speaker's words create the reality she inhabits.

In the same way, we notice at a certain point that our various inferences begin to converge. It is more likely, for instance, that our speaker is a housewife if she is a woman shopping in a supermarket (rather than a woman addressing a jury, or performing heart surgery) and it is more likely that she is shopping in a supermarket if she is a housewife. Our analysis thus demonstrates how certain elements in the passage simultaneously confirm the inferences that (a) the speaker is a woman, (b) the woman is a housewife, and (c) this housewife is shopping in a supermarket.

At this point we are in a position to make certain other inferences about the speaker's present situation: when she was young, she says, she was *miserable* and *poor*. Is there any indication that, having gotten married, she is no longer poor? To answer this question we look again at what she is buying: what interests us now about *wild rice* and *Cornish game hens* is that they are expensive, even fancy, items, precisely the sort of thing that indicate that a shopper is middle class and reasonably well-to-do. (Along with the *station wagon* to which the boy carries her groceries, they also suggest the world not simply of the housewife, but specifically of the suburban middle-class housewife.)

Since the speaker suggests that her being *young* and *miserable* had something to do with her being *poor* (and that when she was young she identified being happy with being married and having money), we are led to ask about her present situation: is she any less miserable now that her wishes have been fulfilled? She says: *What I've become / Troubles me even if I shut my eyes.* She says: *It bewilders me he doesn't see me.* Since a troubled and bewildered woman can scarcely be described as happy, we begin to glimpse a certain relationship between the speaker's youth and her present situation: to have seen her youthful misery as something that could be cured by security and a certain degree of wealth was perhaps a mistake, for now she has those things and is, though in a different way, miserable.

Do any of these inferences allow us to reformulate in more specific terms what we earlier saw as the possibilities of symbolic meaning? Let us look again, for instance, at *Cheer* and *Joy*, which during our analytic reading we said could be taken not simply as brand names but as words describing states of emotion. A moment ago, in connection with the speaker's reference to how *miserable* she was as a girl, we asked if she could be described as presently happy. Our analysis, however, allows us to put the same question in a slightly different way: does the speaker seem *cheer*ful or *joy*ful in her present situation? Since she does not, we raise the possibility that *Cheer* and *Joy* as they occur in line 1 are an ironic commentary on the speaker's present emotional state.

Our analytic reading also suggested that *All* could be taken not simply as a brand name but as a philosophical term: "the totality of what there is"—and that this possibility was strengthened by our discovery that *William James*, with whose writings the speaker is obviously familiar, was a philosopher. Now our analysis of the speaker's present situation leads us to try this meaning in line 9: *I buy All from these shelves.* A series of analytic questions now allows us to see the possibilities of symbolic meaning in more precise terms: is *All* (in the philosophical sense) something that can be bought in stores? Was there a time when the speaker might have thought so?—e.g., when she was *young* and *miserable* and *poor*? Does she think so now?

A full analysis of speaker and situation in "Next Day" would lead to similar questions about other possibilities of symbolic meaning, and would employ precisely the method of analysis we have used in focusing on the symbolic possibilities of *Cheer* and *Joy* and *All*. Since we have at this point taken our analysis of speaker far enough to demonstrate the method involved, we may here step back far enough to observe that the questions we are now asking move us to a new level of inference. Our analysis began, we recall, with certain conclusions deriving directly from our analytic reading: that the speaker was housewife, that she was shopping in a supermarket, etc. When we treat *these* conclusions as proven or established, we may proceed to appeal to them as grounds for further inference: now we are operating, so to speak, at one remove from our analytic reading—our conclusions no longer derive directly from the primary meaning of

Cheer, Joy, All, etc.—and at a more general level of inference.

Yet an analysis of speaker or narrator, though it may soon take us to a very general level of inference—i.e., one where we are able to formulate the possibilities of symbolic meaning in very exact terms—does not lead directly to interpretation. For the speaker of a poem or the narrator of a novel represents only one of the dramatic coordinates of a literary work. Let us now turn to the other, the internal or dramatic audience whom the speaker addresses, and whose presence we must take fully into account when discussing either primary or symbolic meaning.

Both spoken and written language assumes the presence of some sort of audience. The question "Would you mind getting off my foot?" implies a hearer (probably a pretty clumsy one) who is, specifically, standing on the speaker's foot. This is why, when you write a letter, you keep in mind an idea of the person to whom you are writing—your mother, your friend, or whomever. Language communicates, and there is no sense in using it unless there's someone there with whom to communicate.

Now it seems obvious that an author's major objective is to communicate with an audience of readers; we often find poems and novels, in fact, where the author speaks directly to his or her audience. In *Tom Jones*, for instance, which is the first great English novel, Henry Fielding does this frequently. Let's look at a passage where he's explaining that he hasn't felt "obliged to keep even pace with time" (earlier writers of fiction had stuck to a simple time sequence: X happened, then Y happened, etc.):

> My reader then is not to be surprised if, in the course of this work, he shall find some chapters very short, and others altogether as long: some that contain only the time of a single day, and others that comprise years . . . . For as I am, in reality, the founder of a new province of writing, so I am at liberty to make what laws I please therein, and these laws my readers, whom I consider as my subjects, are bound to believe in and obey . . . .

This situation seems clear enough: here is a novelist who, aware that he is telling a story in a way that is unfamiliar to his readers, stops to explain to them what he's doing and why he's doing it.

Even when we have made the necessary distinction between the real Henry Fielding and the imaginary narrator of *Tom Jones* (the voice of the storyteller inside the novel), the situation doesn't seem to change much. The narrator of *Tom Jones* is a novelist (just as the speaker of "When I Have Fears" was a poet), and he is obviously addressing an audience that includes not just the original readers of *Tom Jones*, but you and me as well—in fact, everyone who will ever read the novel.

If we stop and think for a moment, however, this is likely to strike us as a curious notion: how can the narrator of *Tom Jones*, as someone who exists inside the novel, address an audience that is outside the novel? Here, once again, we are confronting the principle that life and literature represent entirely different realities: it doesn't seem possible for Huck Finn or the narrator of *Tom Jones* to talk to you and me, anymore than it's possible for you and me to talk to Huck Finn or the narrator of *Tom Jones*.

If the speaker of a literary work isn't addressing the readers of the work, whom is he addressing? When they encountered this problem, critical theorists soon arrived at an alternative (and logically superior) view of audience. "Since the speaker is someone who exists inside the work," they asked, "doesn't it also make sense to identify an *audience* that exists inside the work, one as different from the real audience of readers as the speaker is from the real author?"

The concept of an internal audience may give you some trouble at first—the speaker, after all, is easy to spot (he's speaking)—but it is another major principle of modern criticism, and one we have to have firmly in mind when we're doing critical interpretation. To see how it works, let's look at the opening lines of a poem we've seen before, "Andrea del Sarto":

> But do not let us quarrel any more,
> No, my Lucrezia; bear with me for once:
> Sit down and all shall happen as you wish.
> You turn your face, but does it bring your heart?

Here it is obvious that Andrea is not talking to you and me, or to an abstract audience of general readers, but to a woman named Lucrezia. As the poem goes on, the dramatic situation becomes clearer: it is evening, and Andrea has finished painting for the day. The woman he is addressing is his wife, a beautiful but selfish woman whose demands on him have destroyed his promise as an artist. In the end, it turns out that Andrea is painting pictures on commission to pay off the gambling debts of one of Lucrezia's illicit lovers.

None of this makes any sense if we assume that Andrea is addressing the actual reader of the poem: we only understand the meaning when we are fully aware of the presence and character of Lucrezia. Lucrezia is the *dramatic audience* in "Andrea del Sarto"—a listener who exists inside the poem in exactly the same sense as Andrea does as speaker. But if Andrea is talking to Lucrezia, what becomes of our role as readers? W. K. Wimsatt, the great literary theorist who gave prominence to the concept of an internal audience, describes it this way: "the actual reader of a poem is something like a reader over another reader's shoulder; he reads through . . . the person to whom the full tone of the poem is addressed in the fictional situation."[1]

If we think about it for a moment, we see that the concept of dramatic audience is really a simple one, following logically from what we have already learned about the imaginary speaker in literature— it is only natural that the speaker of a poem or the narrator of a story should be addressing a specific audience, and that this audience should exist (as he does) inside the work. Yet this is the kind of simple principle that leads very soon to complex possibilities, for the relationship of an imaginary speaker to his imaginary audience is always complicated, and moves us toward the area of symbolic meaning.

Still, a simple awareness of dramatic audience represents a considerable advance in critical technique, and suggests the next practical step in interpretation: after we have identified and characterized the speaker or narrator of a work, we identify and characterize his dramatic audience. It is extremely important, obviously, to do this correctly and precisely—if we think the speaker of a poem is talking to a woman when he's really talking to a male friend, or if we think that he is speaking to a group of adults when he's actually talking to a child, our entire reading of the poem is going to be mistaken. But identifying a dramatic audience really isn't all that hard, and one soon gets to the point where one does it automatically.

The easiest kind of dramatic audience to identify is the single listener who is in the presence of the speaker. This is the case with

1. W. K. Wimsatt and Monroe C. Beardsley, *The Verbal Icon* (Lexington: University of Kentucky Press, 1954), p. xv.

Lucrezia in "Andrea del Sarto," and it is the case in many sonnets and lyric poems. When, for instance, we read the opening lines of Andrew Marvell's "To His Coy Mistress,"

> Had we but world enough, and time,
> This coyness, lady, were no crime.
> We would sit down, and think which way
> To walk, and pass our long love's day.

we know immediately that the dramatic audience is a young woman whom the speaker is going to try to talk into going to bed with him.

Then there is a more generalized kind of dramatic audience. When the narrator of *Tom Jones* addresses his readers in the passage quoted earlier, we don't know anything very particular about the audience he has in mind, only that he suspects they may be uncomfortable with his manner of telling a story, and will need some reassurance before going back to Tom Jones and his adventures. This is one kind of generalized audience—eighteenth- and nineteenth-century novelists were fond of addressing this audience as "gentle reader" or "gentle readers"—but there are others: the sympathetic friend to whom a disappointed lover pours out his heart, the companion to whom a traveler points out the beauty of nature, etc. This sort of dramatic audience may be a single person or a group of people, an imaginary listener or an imaginary reader, and it is present whenever we are aware that the speaker is speaking directly to someone, but we have only a very general idea of what they are like.

Finally, there is a kind of dramatic audience so fully universalized that the speaker, in addressing it, seems simply to be talking out loud. This happens most often in poetry; consider these lines from Wordsworth's sonnet "The World Is Too Much with Us":

> The world is too much with us; late and soon,
> Getting and spending, we lay waste our powers;
> Little we see in Nature that is ours;
> We have given our hearts away, a sordid boon!

Here, there seems to be no audience at all in sight; in fact, we find out later that the speaker is alone ("standing on this pleasant lea") beside the ocean.

If we're attentive enough, however, we can identify the dramatic audience of the sonnet all the same. Suppose we start by observing that the speaker, even though he is alone, seems to be including himself in some sort of community—"the world is too much with *us*," "*we* lay waste *our* powers," "little *we* see in Nature that is *ours*," etc.

Let us assume, then, that the speaker is addressing the other members of this community. Who are they? Because the speaker's "we" is so general a term, it's tempting to say that he is addressing all of mankind. But then we notice that he is talking to a class of people who "lay waste their powers" in "getting and spending"—that is, who are so absorbed in making money and pursuing worldly success that they have gotten out of touch with the world of nature and common humanity. This seems to leave out a lot of mankind— South Sea islanders, for instance, or poor people, or idle aristocrats.

The speaker of Wordsworth's sonnet, then, is addressing a middle-class audience, and specifically those members of it who, despite their potential for human sympathy, have allowed themselves to get caught up in the world of commerce and financial enterprise we associate with the Industrial Age, and who have become dulled and insensitive in the process. (It also seems clear that the speaker, even as he stands apart to admonish them, in some sense considers himself to be a member of this class of people.)

That's still a pretty general audience, but it is much more specific than "mankind" or "humanity at large," and we identify this audience in precisely the same way as we identified Lucrezia in "Andrea del Sarto": by paying close attention to the imaginary listener (in this case, listeners) the speaker seems to have in mind as he talks. If we were writing a critical essay on this sonnet, we might say at some point that the speaker is "addressing the modern age" (as opposed to a simpler time when life was more leisurely and people lived more in harmony with nature). That would be perfectly all right, because we would really mean that the speaker was addressing a specific class of people who symbolize what is wrong with the modern age. And *that* would mean that, having realized that people don't just go down by the ocean and address the modern age, we had begun by identifying the real dramatic audience of the poem.

This is a distinction we make in doing a critical interpretation of every literary work we read: the *actual* audience of "Andrea del Sarto" or *Tom Jones* or "The World is Too Much with Us" consists of everyone who will ever read those works, and of everyone who has already read them. But the *dramatic* audience, which exists only inside the work, is as specific and immutable as the speaker himself.

ANALYSIS AND INTERPRETATION

In this and the "Analysis and Interpretation" sections that follow chapters 3 and 4, an analytic reading of the selections is assumed —that is, you are asked to have completed the detailed analysis of words and syntax discussed in Chapter 1 before going on to more general questions of analysis and interpretation.

Our basic exercise for this chapter is a detailed analysis of speaker and dramatic audience in the selections below. Your aim should be to proceed from the specific—what, in the most literal terms, do we know about this speaker or this audience—to the general: personality, mood, moral character, etc. The questions following each selection are meant to suggest useful lines of inquiry.

MATTHEW ARNOLD

DOVER BEACH

> The sea is calm tonight.
> The tide is full, the moon lies fair
> Upon the straits—on the French coast the light
> Gleams and is gone; the cliffs of England stand,
> Glimmering and vast, out in the tranquil bay.
> Come to the window, sweet is the night air!
> Only, from the long line of spray
> Where the sea meets the moon-blanched land,
> Listen! you hear the grating roar
> Of pebbles which the waves draw back, and fling,
> At their return, up the high strand,
> Begin, and cease, and then again begin,
> With tremulous cadence slow, and bring
> The eternal note of sadness in.
>
> Sophocles long ago
> Heard it on the Aegean, and it brought
> Into his mind the turbid ebb and flow
> Of human misery; we
> Find also in the sound a thought,
> Hearing it by this distant northern sea.
>
> The Sea of Faith
> Was once, too, at the full, and round earth's shore
> Lay like the folds of a bright girdle furled.

But now I only hear
Its melancholy, long, withdrawing roar,
Retreating, to the breath
Of the night wind, down the vast edges drear
And naked shingles of the world.

Ah, love, let us be true
To one another! for the world, which seems
To lie before us like a land of dreams,
So various, so beautiful, so new,
Hath really neither joy, nor love, nor light,
Nor certitude, nor peace, nor help for pain;
And we are here as on a darkling plain
Swept with confused alarms of struggle and flight,
Where ignorant armies clash by night.

Where exactly is the speaker standing as he speaks? What is the
name of "the straits" he is gazing out at? (A map of England showing
the French coast will help you answer this question.) What is the
"distant northern sea" that reminds the speaker of the Aegean? What
are the differences between the "northern sea" and the Aegean? between
the civilization represented by Sophocles and that represented by the
speaker? In what specific aspects does the sea the speaker is observing
resemble the "Sea of Faith" to which the speaker refers in the last part
of the poem? In what way are the speaker's relation to the "distant
northern sea" and his relation to the "Sea of Faith" similar? What is the
relation of the actual scene of the poem to the "darkling plain" where
"ignorant armies clash by night"?

JOHN MILTON

WHEN I CONSIDER HOW MY LIGHT IS SPENT

When I consider how my light is spent
    Ere half my days, in this dark world and wide,
    And that one talent which is death to hide,
    Lodged with me useless, though my soul more bent
To serve therewith my Maker, and present
    My true account, lest he returning chide;
    "Doth God exact day-labor, light denied?"
    I fondly ask; but Patience to prevent
That murmur, soon replies, "God doth not need
    Either man's work or his own gifts; who best
    Bear his mild yoke, they serve him best. His state
Is kingly. Thousands at his bidding speed

And post o'er land and ocean without rest:
They also serve who only stand and wait."

How old (approximately) is the speaker? What is the "light" that
is "spent"? What is "that one talent which is death to hide"? How is
the speaker's age central to his concerns in the poem? The speaker is a
Christian of a specific sort: how does his attitude toward God com-
plicate his sense of his own predicament? How does it help resolve it?
What is the *exact* relation between the personified "Patience" who
speaks in the final six lines of the poem and the speaker whom we hear
in the first seven lines? What is the speaker's final attitude toward his
fate?

JOHN DONNE

From *MEDITATION XVII*

The church is catholic, universal, so are all her actions; all that
she does belongs to all. When she baptizes a child, that action concerns me; for that child is thereby connected to that body which is
my head too, and ingrafted into that body whereof I am a member.
And when she buries a man, that action concerns me: all mankind
is of one author and is one volume; when one man dies, one chapter is not torn out of the book, but translated into a better language;
and every chapter must be so translated. God employs several trans-
lators; some pieces are translated by age, some by sickness, some
by war, some by justice; but God's hand is in every translation, and
his hand shall bind up all our scattered leaves again for that library
where every book shall lie open to one another. As therefore the
bell that rings to a sermon calls not upon the preacher only, but
upon the congregation to come, so this bell calls us all; but how
much more me, who am brought so near the door by this sickness.
There was a contention as far as a suit (in which piety and dignity,
religion and estimation, were mingled) which of the religious orders
should ring to prayers first in the morning; and it was determined
that they should ring first that rose earliest. If we understand aright
the dignity of this bell that tolls for our evening prayer, we would
be glad to make it ours by rising early, in that application, that it
might be ours as well as his whose indeed it is. The bell doth toll
for him that thinks it doth; and though it intermit again, yet from
that minute that that occasion wrought upon him, he is united to
God. Who casts not up his eye to the sun when it rises? but who
takes off his eye from a comet when that breaks out? Who bends
not his ear to any bell which is passing a piece of himself out of

this world? No man is an island, entire of itself; every man is a piece of the continent, a part of the main. If a clod be washed away by the sea, Europe is the less, as well as if a promontory were, as well as if a manor of thy friend's or of thine own were. Any man's death diminishes me because I am involved in mankind, and therefore never send to know for whom the bell tolls; it tolls for thee.

How does the speaker's condition ("me, who am brought so near the door by this sickness") shape his perspective on the relation of mankind to God? What is the speaker's conception of God? How does this determine his conception of the church to which he belongs? What does the speaker's metaphor of book ("all mankind is of one author and is one volume") and translation ("translated into a better language") tell us about his own character and interests? How does the speaker conceive of himself in relation to God and to other men?

ROBERT FROST

ONCE BY THE PACIFIC

The shattered water made a misty din.
Great waves looked over others coming in,
And thought of doing something to the shore
That water never did to land before.
The clouds were low and hairy in the skies,   5
Like locks blown forward in the gleam of eyes.
You could not tell, and yet it looked as if
The shore was lucky in being backed by cliff,
The cliff in being backed by continent;
It looked as if a night of dark intent   10
Was coming, and not only a night, an age.
Someone had better be prepared for rage.
There would be more than ocean-water broken
Before God's last *Put out the Light* was spoken.

To whom is the speaker describing his experience? To whom does *you* in line 7 refer? To whom does *someone* in line 12 refer? How does the speaker conceive of the relationship between nature and God? How has it been affected by the experience described in the poem? How does he expect his own description of this experience to affect the outlook of his audience?

The poem is a *recollection* of an experience—how long ago, approximately, did the experience take place? (when the speaker was a child? a young man? more recently?) How does the sense of temporal distance from the event affect the speaker's attitude toward his audience? How does his awareness of this audience influence the course of his recollection? (At precisely what point in the poem do we become most aware of this influence?)

WILLIAM BLAKE

AND DID THOSE FEET

> And did those feet in ancient time
> Walk upon England's mountains green?
> And was the holy Lamb of God
> On England's pleasant pastures seen?
>
> And did the Countenance Divine
> Shine forth upon our clouded hills?
> And was Jerusalem builded here,
> Among these dark Satanic Mills?
>
> Bring me my Bow of burning gold:
> Bring me my Arrows of desire:
> Bring me my Spear: O clouds unfold!
> Bring me my Chariot of fire!
>
> I will not cease from Mental Fight,
> Nor shall my Sword sleep in my hand,
> Till we have built Jerusalem
> In England's green & pleasant Land.

Are the questions in the first stanza real or rhetorical? Whom does the speaker expect to answer them? What is the speaker's view of the present spiritual state of England? Does he expect his audience to share this view? Whom does *we* refer to in the line "till we have built Jerusalem"?

ANDREW MARVELL

TO HIS COY MISTRESS

> Had we but world enough, and time,
> This coyness, lady, were no crime.
> We would sit down, and think which way
> To walk, and pass our long love's day.
> Thou by the Indian Ganges' side
> Shouldst rubies find; I by the tide

Of Humber would complain. I would
Love you ten years before the flood,
And you should, if you please, refuse
Till the conversion of the Jews.
My vegetable love should grow
Vaster than empires and more slow;
An hundred years should go to praise
Thine eyes, and on thy forehead gaze;
Two hundred to adore each breast,
But thirty thousand to the rest;
An age at least to every part,
And the last age should show your heart.
For, lady, you deserve this state,
Nor would I love at lower rate.
    But at my back I always hear
Time's wingéd chariot hurrying near;
And yonder all before us lie
Deserts of vast eternity.
Thy beauty shall no more be found.
Nor, in thy marble vault, shall sound
My echoing song; then worms shall try
That long-preserved virginity.
And your quaint honor turn to dust,
And into ashes all my lust:
The grave's a fine and private place,
But none, I think, do there embrace.
    Now therefore, while the youthful hue
Sits on thy skin like morning dew,
And while thy willing soul transpires
At every pore with instant fires,
Now let us sport us while we may,
And now, like amorous birds of prey,
Rather at once our time devour
Than languish in his slow-chapped power.
Let us roll all our strength and all
Our sweetness up into one ball,
And tear our pleasures with rough strife
Thorough the iron gates of life:
Thus, though we cannot make our sun
Stand still, yet we will make him run.

Approximately how old is the speaker? the lady he is addressing?

How is their age central to the speaker's concerns? To what social class do the speaker and his listener belong? How does the speaker's language reveal this? What is the "coyness" about which the speaker is complaining? What has his relationship with the lady been like up till now? How does the speaker's argument about the consummation of their affair relate to his vision of "deserts of vast eternity"? What is the meaning of the word "mistress" as it occurs in the title?

T. S. ELIOT

THE LOVE SONG OF J. ALFRED PRUFROCK

Let us go then, you and I,
When the evening is spread out against the sky
Like a patient etherised upon a table;
Let us go, through certain half-deserted streets,
The muttering retreats   5
Of restless nights in one-night cheap hotels
And sawdust restaurants with oyster-shells:
Streets that follow like a tedious argument
Of insidious intent
To lead you to an overwhelming question . . .   10
Oh, do not ask, 'What is it?'
Let us go and make our visit.

In the room the women come and go
Talking of Michelangelo.

The yellow fog that rubs its back upon the window panes,   15
The yellow smoke that rubs its muzzle on the window-panes,
Licked its tongue into the corners of the evening,
Lingered upon the pools that stand in drains,
Let fall upon its back the soot that falls from chimneys,
Slipped by the terrace, made a sudden leap,   20
And seeing that it was a soft October night,
Curled once about the house, and fell asleep.

And indeed there will be time
For the yellow smoke that slides along the street
Rubbing its back upon the window-panes;   25
There will be a time, there will be time
To prepare a face to meet the faces that you meet;
There will be time to murder and create,
And time for all the works and days of hands
That lift and drop a question on your plate;   30

Time for you and time for me,
And time yet for a hundred indecisions,
And for a hundred visions and revisions,
Before the taking of a toast and tea.

In the room the women come and go   35
Talking of Michelangelo.

And indeed there will be time
To wonder, 'Do I dare?' and, 'Do I dare?'
Time to turn back and descend the stair,
With a bald spot in the middle of my hair—   40
(They will say: 'How his hair is growing thin!')
My morning coat, my collar mounting firmly to the chin,
My necktie rich and modest, but asserted by a simple pin—
(They will say: "But how his arms and legs are thin!')
Do I dare   45
Disturb the universe?
In a minute there is time
For decisions and revisions which a minute will reverse.

For I have known them all already, known them all—
Have known the evenings, mornings, afternoons,   50
I have measured out my life with coffee spoons;
I know the voices dying with a dying fall
Beneath the music from a farther room.
    So how should I presume?

And I have known the eyes already, known them all—   55
The eyes that fix you in a formulated phrase,
And when I am formulated, sprawling on a pin,
When I am pinned and wriggling on the wall,
Then how should I begin
To spit out all the butt-ends of my days and ways?   60
    And how should I presume?

And I have known the arms already, known them all—
Arms that are braceleted and white and bare
(But in the lamplight, downed with light brown hair!)
Is it perfume from a dress   65
That makes me so digress?
Arms that lie along a table, or wrap about a shawl.
    And should I then presume?

And how should I begin?

. . . . .

Shall I say, I have gone at dusk through narrow streets   70
And watched the smoke that rises from the pipes
Of lonely men in shirt-sleeves, leaning out of windows? . . .

I should have been a pair of ragged claws
Scuttling across the floors of silent seas

. . . . .

And the afternoon, the evening, sleeps so peacefully!   75
Smoothed by long fingers,
Asleep . . . tired . . . or it malingers,
Stretched on the floor, here beside you and me.
Should I, after tea and cakes and ices,
Have the strength to force the moment to its crisis?   80
But though I have wept and fasted, wept and prayed,
Though I have seen my head (grown slightly bald) brought
      in upon a platter,
I am no prophet—and here's no great matter;
I have seen the moment of my greatness flicker,
And I have seen the eternal Footman hold my coat, and
      snicker,   85
And in short, I was afraid.

And would it have been worth it, after all,
After the cups, the marmalade, the tea,
Among the porcelain, among some talk of you and me,
Would it have been worth while,   90
To have bitten off the matter with a smile,
To have squeezed the universe into a ball
To roll it towards some overwhelming question,
To say: 'I am Lazarus, come from the dead,
Come back to tell you all, I shall tell you all'—   95
If one, settling a pillow by her head,
   Should say: 'That is not what I meant at all.
   That is not it, at all.'
And would it have been worth it, after all,
Would it have been worth while,   100
After the sunsets and the dooryards and the sprinkled streets,

After the novels, after the teacups, after the skirts that trail
      along the floor—
And this, and so much more?—

It is impossible to say just what I mean!
But as if a magic lantern threw the nerves in patterns on a
    screen: 105
Would it have been worth while
If one, settling a pillow or throwing off a shawl,
And turning toward the window, should say:
   'That is not it at all,
   That is not what I meant, at all.'   110

     . . . . .

No! I am not Prince Hamlet, nor was meant to be;
Am an attendant lord, one that will do
To swell a progress, start a scene or two,
Advise the prince; no doubt, an easy tool,
Deferential, glad to be of use,   115
Politic, cautious, and meticulous;
Full of high sentence, but a bit obtuse;
At times, indeed, almost ridiculous—
Almost, at times, the Fool.

I grow old . . .I grow old . . .   120
I shall wear the bottoms of my trousers rolled.

Shall I part my hair behind? Do I dare to eat a peach?
I shall wear white flannel trousers, and walk upon the beach.
I have heard the mermaids singing, each to each.

I do not think that they will sing to me.   125

I have seen them riding seaward on the waves
Combing the white hair of the waves blown back
When the wind blows the water white and black.

We have lingered in the chambers of the sea
By sea-girls wreathed with seaweed red and brown   130
Till human voices wake us, and we drown.

How do we know that the speaker of the poem is a male? What is his relationship to the "women" of lines 13 and 35? To the women described in lines 62–67?

Is the dramatic audience of the poem male or female? What is the relationship between the *you* of lines 1 (*Let us go then, you and I*), 27 (*To prepare a face to meet the faces that you meet*), and 89 (*Among the porcelain, among some talk of you and me*)? Does *you* in every case refer to the audience the speaker is addressing? If not, whom is he addressing?

What does the speaker's description of the evening as "spread out against the sky / Like a patient etherised upon a table" tell us about his mood? What sort of world does Prufrock normally inhabit (see lines 49–66)? What is the relation of that world to the world of "one-night cheap hotels / And sawdust restaurants" described at the beginning of the poem (and again in lines 70–72)? What is Prufrock's precise relation to each? What does this tell us about him?

What is the "overwhelming question" mentioned in line 10? Is it the same "question" referred to in line 30?

In lines 92–93, Prufrock echoes some lines from Marvell's "To His Coy Mistress":

> Let us roll all our strength and all
> Our sweetness up into one ball,
> And tear our pleasures with rough strife
> Thorough the iron gates of life.

As an experiment, try reading this part of the poem as the utterance of a modern lover who does not have the courage of the speaker of "To His Coy Mistress"—that is, the courage to put the "overwhelming question" to his lady—and whose sense of his own failure brings Marvell's poem to his mind. How does this allow us to explain the meaning of lines 86–103? In literal terms, what action is Prufrock imagining in those lines? Where is he when he utters them?

In "To His Coy Mistress," the speaker says:

> But at my back I always hear
> Time's wingéd chariot hurrying near;
> And yonder all before us lie
> Deserts of vast eternity.

Prufrock says:

> I have seen the moment of my greatness flicker,
> And I have seen the eternal Footman hold my coat, and snicker,
> And in short, I was afraid.

What, approximately, is Prufrock's age? How does his age relate to his sense of spiritual dilemma (see lines 120–125)? What does the relationship between sexual consummation and human mortality in Marvell's poem suggest about Prufrock's dilemma (see the two passages quoted directly above).

Who are the *mermaids* referred to in line 124? When Prufrock says *We have lingered in the chambers of the sea* (line 129), to whom does *we* refer? Whom is Prufrock addressing at the end of the poem?

In answering the above questions, and in eliciting whatever other information you consider pertinent about speaker and audience, you will have compiled a rough set of analytic notes on each selection. These notes may be taken as the raw material for a short interpretive exercise: in any two of the selections above, account *either* for the relation of the speaker's situation and personality to the way he views the world *or* for the way the presence of the dramatic audience influences the speaker's perception of the world. Although you need not include everything from your notes, anything you omit should be consistent with your analysis of speaker and audience, and your description of the speaker's view of the world should suggest something about the total meaning of the selection.

3
SYMBOLIC MEANING

The nature of the internal relationship between speaker and audience underlies a central principle of literary interpretation, the principle that poems and novels and plays portray an imaginary reality that in a sense has little connection with the "real" world. A work of literature exists *in* the real world, of course—if it didn't, none of us could read it—but the possibility of criticism begins in our recognition that it also exists apart from our world. This is what the philosopher Ernst Cassirer meant when he described the literary work as "a self-contained cosmos with its own center of gravity." When we interpret a work, we are really exploring this cosmos, and trying to discover exactly where the center of gravity lies.

An analysis of speaker and audience, we have seen, is analysis not of symbolic meaning but of the special coordinates within which symbolic meaning occurs in literature. Now we are ready to consider the stage of literary analysis that immediately precedes the interpretation of symbolic meaning—analysis of *tone*. As a technical term in literary criticism, tone has a very precise definition: it is *the attitude adopted by the speaker when addressing his dramatic audience.* Although this may seem a simple enough concept, it is a very important one, for in it we have for the first time a principle encompassing the entire dramatic situation portrayed in the work—not only the speaker's attitude toward his dramatic audience, but his attitude toward himself and his own situation.

Analysis of tone plays a major role in interpretation, however, because tone involves something much larger than attitude: it involves a conception of self. One way of illustrating this principle is to think about the roles all of us play in real life: when you are talking to your roommate, for instance, you speak and behave differently than when you are talking to your chemistry professor, or when you are discussing your blood pressure with your doctor, or when you are being interviewed for a job. In each case, you're placed in a different role, which means that for the moment you conceive of yourself in a different way—as a roommate, chemistry student, medical patient, or job applicant.

The dramatic situation portrayed in a poem or novel isn't exactly like any of these real-life situations, but the two do have something in common. When we talk about the tone of a literary work, we are talking about (1) the way the speaker conceives of himself at any given moment, and (2) the way his self-conception is influenced by the presence of the imaginary audience he is addressing. Tone is easiest to isolate and characterize when the speaker is in a conventional and well-defined role—if he is a smitten young man addressing a beautiful young woman, for instance, we know that he conceives of himself as a lover, and we can guess pretty much what he is going to say—and it is most difficult to characterize when the speaker is addressing a generalized audience, but the principle is the same in every case.

We shall discuss, later on, how the speaker's conception of himself determines his view of the world, but for the moment let us explore the concept of tone in a little more detail. Every literary work pictures a unique dramatic situation—i.e., a speaker in a unique relationship to his dramatic audience—so no two works can have precisely the same tone. Still, many literary works portray roughly similar dramatic situations (the Renaissance, for instance, produced hundreds of sonnets in which despairing lovers plead with cold-hearted mistresses), and these similarities allow us to make certain general observations.

The least difficult kind of dramatic situation with which to deal is one in which the speaker's relationship to his audience remains consistent from beginning to end. There may be variations of mood within the situation, but these present no great problem: a lover may go from pleading with his mistress to chastizing her for being so hard-hearted, but he remains a lover, she a mistress. We find this consistency of tone in many works, from those with well-defined dramatic audiences to those with very generalized ones. Here are some lines from Shelley's sonnet "England in 1819":

> An old, mad, blind, despised, and dying king;
> Princes, the dregs of their dull race, who flow
> Through public scorn,—mud from a muddy spring;
> Rulers who neither see nor feel nor know,
> But leechlike to their fainting country cling
> Till they drop, blind in blood, without a blow . . . .

The speaker in this sonnet is an angry radical describing an unbearable situation. Do we, then, simply characterize his tone as "angry" and let it go at that? We might, but only if we hadn't taken the trouble to figure out the dramatic situation.

Let's start with the obvious question: who is the dramatic audience? The speaker is angry *at* the corrupt and useless rulers of his country, and if he were speaking *to* them (that is, if they were the dramatic audience), we could properly describe his tone as angry. But he isn't: he's talking *about* them to someone else, his real dramatic audience. The speaker's anger does, however, define this audience for us: as a radical who has stood apart from society and seen how bad things really are, he's addressing those who have just let themselves drift complacently along, never realizing that their world is on the brink of upheaval. The speaker isn't angry at this audience, but he's trying to communicate his anger to them, to wake them up.

How, then, do we describe the speaker's tone? In this case it's a bit complicated, but I can give you a rough idea of how we might go about it. Basically, we might observe, the speaker is admonishing his audience for their blindness. But he is doing more than that: he is admonishing them in exactly the same way as the Old Testament prophets admonished the faithful for their tolerance of a world that had grown corrupt, and he is implicitly warning that some sort of cataclysm will occur if things don't change:

> Religion Christless, Godless—a book sealed;
> A Senate—Time's worst statute unrepealed—
> Are graves from which a glorious Phantom may
> Burst, to illumine our tempestuous day.

The Phantom here is not Divine retribution but political revolution—the retribution of the oppressed—but essentially our young radical has placed himself in a prophetic role, and we thus describe his tone as prophetic.

Shelley's sonnet is a good example of a dramatic situation in which the speaker's relationship to his audience remains consistent throughout. This frequently happens in longer works as well, and in such cases we can describe the speaker's tone fairly economically. But there are also works in which the tone changes in some important way, and in these we have to look for an underlying change in the dramatic situation. Here is a passage from Dickens's novel *Bleak House*, where the narrator is describing one Mrs. Bagnet (whom her husband calls "the old girl"), an honest, open-hearted soldier's wife:

> The old girl's umbrella is of a flabby habit of waist, and seems to be in need of stays—an appearance that is possibly referable to its having served, through a series of years, at home as a cupboard, and on journeys as a carpet bag. She never puts it up . . . but generally uses the instrument as a wand with which to point out joints of meat or bunches of greens in marketing, or to arrest the attention of tradesmen by a friendly poke.

Here the narrator of *Bleak House* appears as a good-natured storyteller speaking to an audience whom he expects to share his comic enjoyment of Mrs. Bagnet's minor eccentricities. But observe how his tone changes later in the story when he has finished describing the death of Little Jo, a poverty-stricken orphan whom society has made an outcast:

> The light is come upon the dark benighted way. Dead!
> Dead, your Majesty. Dead, my lords and gentlemen. Dead, Right and Wrong Reverends of every order. Dead, men and

women, born with Heavenly compassion in your hearts. And dying thus around us, every day!

This is an impassioned social statement, and in making it the narrator has shifted his gaze to an audience within an audience: the Queen, who is so removed from her people that she cannot see the suffering of the poor, the lords and gentlemen who are so occupied with their own business that they are oblivious to poverty, clergymen who go around acting pious and have forgotten that real religion begins in charity, ordinary people who may go to Church on Sunday but never think of the plight of creatures like Little Jo.

These two passages from *Bleak House* illustrate what literary critics call a modulation in tone—that is, although the narrator goes from being a good-natured storyteller to an angry social critic, we are always aware of the close relationship between his two roles. This happens frequently in literature, and is something with which we must always be prepared to deal when we are doing critical interpretation. Our technique, however, is only an extension of our original method: we isolate the speaker's basic relationship to his audience, then watch attentively for significant adjustments within that relationship.

Finally, at the other extreme from the consistent speaker-audience relationship, there are dramatic situations in which tone shifts so drastically that the relationship in effect breaks down. Let's look at the beginning of Nabokov's *Pale Fire*, which is really a novel, but which is in the form of a long poem by a poet named John Shade, with an introduction and notes by a scholar named Dr. Kinbote:

> *Pale Fire*, a poem in heroic couplets, of nine hundred ninety-nine lines, divided into four cantos, was composed by John Francis Shade (born July 5, 1898, died July 21, 1959) during the last twenty days of his life . . . . A methodical man, John Shade usually copied out his daily quota of completed lines at midnight but even if he recopied them again later, as I suspect he sometimes did, he marked his card or cards not with the date of his final adjustments, but with that of his Corrected Draft or first Fair Copy. I mean, he preserved the date of actual creation rather than that of second or third thoughts. There is a very loud amusement park right in front of my present lodgings.

In this case, the narrator goes from being a somewhat pedestrian scholar to a noise-distracted lodger all in the space of a few sentences. What bothers us here is the abrupt change of roles: we do not expect someone writing a learned introduction to a poem suddenly to complain about what is going on outside his window. How, then, do we describe his tone? Reading on a little farther helps, but we can guess the answer from the passage we have just read: Kinbote is insane, and he reveals his insanity when he shows himself incapable of addressing one dramatic audience at a time.

Most often, we shall be working somewhere between the two extremes suggested by "England in 1819" and *Pale Fire*, where the speaker-audience relationship is neither radically consistent nor radically inconsistent, and where minor adjustments in the speaker's attitude are revealed as modulations in tone. The principle is the same, however, for every work: in accounting for tone we have accounted for the entire dramatic situation pictured in the work, and have gone a long way toward finding our way into the world of the poem or story we are reading.

Once we have analyzed the tone of a passage, or the modulations of tone in an entire work, we are ready to interpret its symbolic meaning. This is the real subject of literary criticism, and most of the critical terms we shall now encounter (image, metaphor, theme, etc.) exist to deal with it. Once we have learned the critical principles already discussed there is no need to be dismayed by these terms, or by the mysterious facility with which literary critics seem to use them: the terms are indispensable, each one has a precise meaning, and with use they soon become entirely natural. Since everything we are going to discuss now takes place within the familiar context of speaker, audience, and dramatic situation, our interpretation of symbolic meaning will involve many of the same principles we have already learned. Now, however, we are at last prepared to make conclusive rather than tentative statements about symbolic meaning.

Our method of literary analysis allows us, once we have analyzed tone, to see in very precise terms how the speaker of a poem or the narrator of a novel conceives of himself. As we have seen all along, this involves a process of indirect implication: if speakers and narrators simply told us how they conceived of themselves, there wouldn't be any need for analysis—they would simply say "I am a disappointed lover" or "I am an ironic observer of human folly," and our work would be done for us. Literature would be pretty dull if this happened, but in fact it doesn't. What happens is something much more complex: a speaker reveals the way he conceives himself through his tone, in the act of addressing his dramatic audience.

Now we encounter a crucial distinction: the way a speaker conceives of himself isn't necessarily the way he is. Literature is full of speakers who think they are wits when they're actually dullards, or who see themselves as wise and perceptive when they're really silly and oblivious. Here, for instance, is Holofernes, a character in Shakespeare's *Love's Labours Lost* who thinks of himself as a very learned man. The company has just been hunting, and someone has said that the deer they killed was a buck:

> *Holofernes.* Sir Nathaniel, *haud credo.* [Latin: "I don't be-lieve it."]
> *Dull.* 'Twas not a haud credo; 'twas a pricket. ["young buck"]
> *Holofernes.* Most barbarous intimation! yet a kind of insinua-tion, as it were, *in via*, in way, of explication; *facere*, as it were, replication, or rather, *ostentare*, to show, as it were, his inclination, after his undressed, unpolished, uneducated, unpruned, untrained, or rather, unlettered, or ratherest, unconfirmed fashion, to assert my *haud credo* a deer.

We can see that Holofernes is not learned at all, that he is simply a foolish pedant with a big ego. But observe that the comedy begins in Holofernes's conception of himself: he isn't just a fool with a smattering of book learning who is trying to pass himself off as an accomplished scholar—he actually thinks he *is* one. Holofernes is a character in a play, but if he were the narrator of a story, we would be dealing with an entire world as it was viewed by a pedant who thought of himself as a genuinely wise and learned man.

One of the ways in which speakers reveal their view of the world involves meaning that is not literal but symbolic—that is, they look at the world in such a way that the objects and events of everyday experience become associated in their minds with something that is more abstract: a rose with beauty, darkness with death, springtime with youth, and so on. This is what allows us, as literary critics, to say that a poem that mostly concerns roses is really a poem about beauty.

Symbolism is a pretty complicated subject, but on the level we have to deal with it (as literary critics, not philosophers of language), it isn't so mysterious. Let's start at the primary level, the one people have in mind when they say that language itself is symbolic. This simply means that the *a, b, c, d* (etc.) of our alphabet can be arranged in combinations that "stand for" something in the real world. The combination *cugzlat* isn't a symbol of anything at all—it is just a bunch of letters arranged in a meaningless sequence. But the combination *tree* is a symbol—it "stands for" something green and leafy and growing, with roots and branches and twigs.

The critical term that is used to refer to this kind of symbolic meaning is *image*. It is perfectly correct to say that the word *tree* is an image of the thing with roots and branches that it represents, but usually we use image to refer to a more extended kind of description. Here is a descriptive passage from Oliver Goldsmith's "The Deserted Village":

> How often have I paused on every charm,
> The sheltered cot, the cultivated farm,
> The never-failing brook, the busy mill,
> The decent church that topped the neighboring hill,
> The hawthorn bush, with seats beneath the shade . . . .

An image is something that represents in words an idea of the real world, the one that's filled with things we see and hear and taste and smell and touch. We can use the word image to refer to anything from an isolated bit of description ("the image of the rose in line 2") to the scene portrayed in an entire work ("Hemingway's image of expatriate Paris"). For images are themselves created out of images: when we speak of Goldsmith's image of an English village, we are implicitly referring to all the elements of his description: brook, mill, cottages, farms, etc.

When we talk about an image, we're still at a fairly rudimentary level of symbolic meaning, one where the word *brook* simply stands for a meandering current of running water. There is a more complicated level, however, which occupies most of our attention when we are doing critical interpretation. As an example, let's look closely at a passage from Tennyson's poem "Ulysses." The dramatic situation is this: Ulysses was the hero of Homer's *Odyssey*, a great epic poem that tells of his perilous ten-year voyage home to Ithaca after the

Trojan War. In Tennyson's poem, after having quietly ruled his island kingdom for a number of years, he has grown restless. We hear him addressing the companions who were with him on his voyage:

> I cannot rest from travel; I will drink
> Life to the lees. All times I have enjoyed
> Greatly, have suffered greatly, both with those
> That loved me, and alone; on shore, and when
> Through scudding drifts the rainy Hyades
> Vexed the dim sea. I am become a name;
> For always roaming with a hungry heart
> Much have I seen and known—cities of men
> And manners, climates, councils, governments,
> Myself not least, but honored of them all—
> And drunk delight of battle with my peers,
> Far on the ringing plains of windy Troy.

We can figure out the tone of this passage without much trouble: Ulysses obviously has a heroic conception of himself, and it is revealed now because he is trying to inspire his old companions ("my mariners, Souls that have toiled, and wrought, and thought with me") with his own renewed sense of high adventure and noble purpose. But the meaning of the poem finally concerns Ulysses' view of the world, and uncovering that demands a special kind of analysis.

Ulysses' speech is filled with images: voyage, battle, cities, climates, councils, governments. But not all these images are of the simple descriptive type we found in Goldsmith: some have a *figurative* meaning—that is, they point beyond their literal meaning to something more abstract and complex. Let's look more carefully at Ulysses' assertion in line 6: "I will drink life to the lees."

This is a *metaphor*. There is no logical way for anyone to "drink life"—drinking is something you can do only with liquids, and life is not a liquid. Still, we seem to know what Ulysses means by this— he is determined to live his life out actively, not to give in to old age until he finally has to die. This is our second level of symbolic meaning, the one that most precisely reveals the speaker's view of the world.

Metaphor is usually defined as a figure of speech in which one thing (X) is identified with another thing (Y). This $X = Y$ formula is all right, as long as we realize that it covers a lot of very complicated situations. There is, however, nothing very complicated about metaphor itself; we use it all the time. If you're angry at someone and you say "Sam is a real ass," you've just used the basic formula: Sam, a human male (X), is a donkey (Y). We don't mean, presumably, that Sam actually *is* a donkey, only that he shares some of the less attractive characteristics of the species.

This is precisely what happens in literary metaphor. We have talked a bit about how poets are always comparing women to roses; let's look at two standard examples. In a poem by Edmund Spenser, the speaker praises a woman by saying

> She is the rose, the glory of the day.

This, too, fulfills the basic formula: she (X) is a rose (Y). Now let's look at a closely related kind of symbolic figure. The speaker of Robert Burns's "A Red, Red Rose" begins his description of his sweetheart like this:

> Oh my love's like a red, red rose,
> That's newly sprung in June . . . .

This second example is a *simile*, a figure of speech in which the speaker says that "X is *like* Y" instead of "X equals Y." When we are analyzing symbolic meaning, metaphor and simile are the only really indispensable terms. There are many different kinds of metaphor and simile, and some of them have fancy names (synecdoche, metonymy, etc.) left over from the days when scholars wrote elaborate rhetorical handbooks. Although it's nice to know what synecdoche is when we run into it, it is not essential: we can do literary criticism perfectly well just by using the terms metaphor and simile.

When we are doing literary interpretation, however, we have to look beyond these simple formulas ($X=Y$, X is like Y) to the process that gives them meaning. No one can just go around randomly asserting that X is Y: if I were to come up to you on the street and earnestly announce that "Your foot is a zebra," you'd probably call the nearest psychiatric clinic. There has to be a context that controls the relationship of X and Y. This is why, when a lover compares his mistress to a rose, we know that certain things about roses are relevant to the comparison (that they are fragile, delicate, beautiful) and that other things are not (that they need fertilizer, have to be watered once a week, etc.).

The context that gives meaning to metaphor and simile is the consciousness of the speaker, and in dealing with these we return to matters we have already discussed: speaker-audience relationship, view of the world, and so on. When someone in a poem or a novel or a play says that X is Y, it means that certain similarities between X and Y have suddenly become so apparent to him that he has forgotten the differences between them—he is actually *seeing* X as Y. Simile involves a similar process, except that it's more self-conscious: in taking the time to say that X is *like* Y, the speaker is showing that he is still aware of the differences. So both metaphor and simile refer us back to the speaker, and both reveal in great detail something about the speaker's conception of the world.

Let's go back to Ulysses' speech, and see exactly what his use of metaphor tells us about him. The sentence we have already talked about is, in fact, pretty complicated: "I will drink life to the lees." Here there is no obvious $X = Y$ formula, as there was in "She is the rose," and we have to do some work to identify the X and Y. The crucial phrase, we agreed, is *drink life*—since drinking is something we can do only with beverages, it's clear that Ulysses is in some sense saying that life (X) is a beverage (Y). (That may sound pretty silly, but let's let it go for a second.) This is an example of *implicit metaphor*, a kind of metaphor where the X and Y are somewhat disguised by the syntax. It occurs frequently in literature (more often than the simple variety, in fact) and it demands all our powers of critical concentration to contend with.

If Ulysses were only saying that life is a beverage, his image *would* be pretty silly, but there is more to the metaphor than that: what he is really invoking is the picture of a man at a banquet who drains his cup of wine to the bottom (*lees* refers to the sediment that collects at the bottom of the cup). In this sense, his determination to *drink life to the lees* is a determination to experience everything he can before dying. Once we have figured this out, another line in Ulysses' speech is likely to strike us:

> For always roaming with a hungry heart
> Much have I seen and known . . . .

This is another implicit metaphor: a "heart" cannot be "hungry," because hunger is something that involves food, and a heart doesn't eat food. Even when we have translated the metaphor into a more plausible form—"I have a heart that is hungry in the same sense that people hunger for food"—we still have to uncover the X and Y terms. Actually, the simple phrase *hungry heart* contains *two* metaphors, and to make real sense of it we have to untangle it as follows: "I have a heart (X) that is hungry for experience (X^1) in the same way that people (Y) hunger for food (Y^1)."

That may sound pretty complicated, but we have little trouble uncovering the metaphor: "experience is the food of the heart." What is striking about this is that it so obviously resembles Ulysses' earlier image of "drinking life"—food and drink are very closely related, and in both cases they are being compared to experience. When we have this in mind, another metaphor further on in the speech stands out in sharp relief; I have traveled far and wide, Ulysses says,

> And drunk delight of battle with my peers,
> Far on the ringing plains of windy Troy.

At this point, the phrase that is likely to catch our attention is *drunk delight of battle.* The event Ulysses has in mind is the Trojan War, where he fought alongside other Greek kings and princes against the Trojans, but it is only from the metaphor that we know how he looks back on the experience. Again, we have to do some work to uncover the X and Y: "to me, the experience of battle (X) is like a delightful beverage (Y)"—in this case, like a heady and intoxicating beverage, the kind a man would drink when he was at a banquet with his friends. Once again we are in a metaphoric situation where experience is being compared to food and drink.

Now let's step back for a moment and see what Ulysses' metaphors reveal about his perception of the world. Each of the metaphors involves a certain kind of symbolic meaning, but together they develop a pattern of symbolic meaning, something that strongly indicates the kind of order Ulysses perceives in existence.

When Ulysses repeatedly compares experience to food and drink, it is obvious that he has a specific kind of experience in mind: he's not talking about the things that people do routinely (walking the dog, weeding the garden) but about certain extraordinary situations (dangerous voyages, battles). Now, eating and drinking *are* activities that we perform routinely: they exist at the most basic level of life, and if we didn't do them we'd die. That's the important thing about the metaphoric pattern we have discovered in Ulysses' discourse: he's not simply saying that experience is the food of the spirit, but that without a constant seeking after experience, real and meaningful experience, the spirit dies.

Actually, Ulysses isn't *saying* any of this: there is no place in the poem where he stops and announces that "experience is the sustenance of the human spirit, and without it the spirit dies." All this belongs to the way Ulysses looks at life, to the way he conceives of himself and the world, and the symbolic dimension of his discourse is something we understand only when we concentrate fully on what his spontaneous use of metaphor reveals about him. This concern with symbolic meaning is what literary criticism is ultimately all about.

ANALYSIS AND INTERPRETATION

The first four selections in this section ask you to expand your analysis of speaker and audience to account for tone: what attitude does the speaker adopt when addressing his audience? how does his conception of his audience define the way he conceives of himself? how does the speaker's tone shape the meaning of his utterance?

The next four selections ask for a full analysis of symbolic meaning, and answers to the questions following them might take the form of a two-page interpretive essay incorporating specific observations about speaker, audience, tone, and dramatic situation. It should be emphasized that such questions represent only what might be called an angle of inquiry, and that they ideally converge on a full interpretation of the work.

A. E. HOUSMAN

EPITAPH ON AN ARMY OF MERCENARIES

These, in the day when heaven was falling,
    The hour when earth's foundations fled,
Followed their mercenary calling
    And took their wages and are dead.

Their shoulders held the sky suspended;
    They stood, and earth's foundations stay;
What God abandoned, these defended,
    And saved the sum of things for pay.

3. SYMBOLIC MEANING

How does the narrator view the scene he is describing? How does he think his audience views it? How does the assumed divergence of views help explain the tone of the poem? How does the narrator expect his words to affect the attitude of his audience? What does this tell us about the way he conceives of his audience? What does it tell us about the way he conceives of himself? How, briefly, might we characterize the tone of the poem?

HUGH MACDIARMID

ANOTHER EPITAPH ON AN ARMY OF MERCENARIES

It is a God-damned lie to say that these
Saved, or knew, anything worth any man's pride.
They were professional murderers and they took
Their blood money and impious risks and died.
In spite of all their kind some elements of worth   5
With difficulty persist here and there on earth.

Suppose that the single existing copy of Housman's "Epitaph on an Army of Mercenaries" had been destroyed immediately after being read by the speaker of this poem. How should we know, from reading this poem *only*, what the speaker is replying to? Whom should we say he is accusing of having told a "God-damned lie"? What is the *exact* force of "God-damned" in this context?

Why does the speaker conceive of his antagonist as having told a *lie*—i.e., a deliberate falsehood? How does he conceive of his antagonist's relation to the "professional murderers" of line 3? How is his audience supposed to react to "their kind"? (What is the exact meaning of *kind* in this context?) What attitudes must the audience adopt before the speaker will be prepared to recognize his kinship with them? How does this expectation influence the tone of the poem?

THOMAS WYATT

THEY FLEE FROM ME

They flee from me, that sometime did me seek,
With naked foot stalking in my chamber.
I have seen them, gentle, tame, and meek,
That now are wild, and do not remember
That sometime they put themselves in danger
To take bread at my hand; and now they range,
Busily seeking with a continual change.

Thanked be fortune it hath been otherwise,
Twenty times better; but one in special,

In thin array, after a pleasant guise,
When her loose gown from her shoulders did fall,
And she me caught in her arms long and small,
And therewithall sweetly did me kiss
And softly said, "Dear heart, how like you this?"

It was no dream, I lay broad waking.
But all is turned, thorough my gentleness,
Into a strange fashion of forsaking;
And I have leave to go, of her goodness,
And she also to use newfangleness.
But since that I so kindely am served,
I fain would know what she hath deserved.

Who are the *they* referred to in the first line? What is their relation to the *she* of the second stanza? To whom is the speaker describing his disappointing experience? What is his attitude toward the women he is describing? How does he expect his audience to feel toward them? Is his audience male or female (or both)? How does the speaker's description of the women (*stalking, gentle, tame, meek*) define his conception of them, and of himself? How is the audience supposed to answer the question asked in the last two lines? How does this define their relationship to the speaker? How might we briefly characterize the speaker's tone?

SIR THOMAS MALORY

From MORTE DARTHUR

Then Sir Bedivere departed and went to the sword and lightly took it up, and so he went to the water's side; and there he bound the girdle about the hilts, and threw the sword as far into the water as he might. And there came an arm and an hand above the water and took it and clutched it, and shook it thrice and brandished; and then vanished away the hand with the sword into the water. So Sir Bedivere came again to the King and told him what he saw.

"Alas," said the King, "help me hence, for I dread me I have tarried overlong."

Then Sir Bedivere took the King upon his back and so went with him to that water's side. And when they were at the water's side, even fast by the bank hoved a little barge with many fair ladies in it; and among them all was a queen; and all they had black hoods, and all they wept and shrieked when they saw King Arthur.

"Now put me into that barge," said the King; and so he did softly. And there received him three ladies with great mourning, and so they set them down. And in one of their laps King Arthur laid his head, and then the queen said, "Ah, my dear brother, why have ye tarried so long from me? Alas, this wound on your head hath caught overmuch cold." And anon they rowed fromward the land, and Sir Bedivere beheld all the ladies go froward him.

Then Sir Bedivere cried and said, "Ah, my lord Arthur, what shall become of me, now ye go from me and leave me here alone among mine enemies?"

"Comfort thyself," said the King, "and do as well as thou mayest, for in me is no trust for to trust in. For I must into the vale of Avilion to heal me of my grievous wound. And if thou hear nevermore of me, pray for my soul."

Does the narrator assume that his audience already knows something about King Arthur and his adventures, or that they are now learning about him for the first time? How does this assumption influence his description of events? When are those events assumed to have taken place? (in the immediate past? in the distant past?) How does the temporal distance separating the narrator and his audience from King Arthur's reign influence his description? How does the narrator conceive of his relation to his audience? How might we briefly characterize his tone?

GREGORY CORSO

DREAM OF A BASEBALL STAR

I dreamed Ted Williams
leaning at night
against the Eiffel Tower, weeping.

He was in uniform
and his bat lay at his feet   5
—knotted and twiggy.

'Randall Jarrell says you're a poet!' I cried.
'So do I! I say you're a poet!'

He picked up his bat with blown hands;
stood there astraddle as he would in the batter's box,   10
and laughed! flinging his schoolboy wrath
toward some invisible pitcher's mound
—waiting the pitch all the way from heaven.

It came; hundreds came! all afire!
He swung and swung and swung and connected not one   15
sinker curve hook or right-down-the-middle.
A hundred strikes!
The umpire dressed in strange attire
thundered his judgement: YOU'RE OUT!
And the phantom crowd's horrific boo   20
dispersed the gargoyles from Notre Dame.

And I screamed in my dream:
God! throw thy merciful pitch!
Herald the crack of bats!
Hooray the sharp liner to left!   25
Yea the double, the triple!
Hosannah the home run!

    1. What elements of the poem tell us that this is a waking recol-
lection of a dream? How do the "dream elements" function symbolically in this context?

    2. How is Ted Williams, as a dream figure, related to the speaker
himself? What is the symbolic relationship of baseball to poetry in the
poem? In what sense is the baseball player's plight the plight of a poet?

    3. How is the phantasmagoric baseball world of the poem (the
"invisible pitcher's mound," "the umpire dressed in strange attire," the
"phantom crowd," etc.) related symbolically to the more ordinary world
of Paris ("the Eiffel Tower," "the gargoyles from Notre Dame," etc.)?
What is the *actual* relationship between the world of American major
league baseball and Paris considered as a cultural symbol?

WALLACE STEVENS

ANECDOTE OF THE JAR

        I placed a jar in Tennessee,
        And round it was, upon a hill.
        It made the slovenly wilderness
        Surround that hill.

        The wilderness rose up to it,
        And sprawled around, no longer wild.
        The jar was round upon the ground
        And tall and of a port in air.

        It took dominion everywhere.
        The jar was grey and bare.

> It did not give of bird or bush,
> Like nothing else in Tennessee.

1. Explain the precise symbolic relationship between the "round" jar and the "slovenly" wilderness. (How does the word *slovenly* help us define this relationship in precise terms? What are the pertinent connotative meanings of *slovenly* that allow us to do so?)

2. Explain how the relationship between jar and wilderness is determined by the jar's being "placed" on the hill by the speaker. What does the speaker's description of the result—"it took dominion everywhere"—tell us about his perception of civilization and untamed nature? What is this perception?

WILLIAM WORDSWORTH

THE SOLITARY REAPER

> Behold her, single in the field,
> Yon solitary Highland Lass!
> Reaping and singing by herself;
> Stop here, or gently pass!
> Alone she cuts and binds the grain,
> And sings a melancholy strain;
> O listen! for the Vale profound
> Is overflowing with the sound.
>
> No Nightingale did ever chaunt
> More welcome notes to weary bands
> Of travelers in some shady haunt,
> Among Arabian sands;
> A voice so thrilling ne'er was heard
> In springtime from the Cuckoo bird,
> Breaking the silence of the seas
> Among the farthest Hebrides.
>
> Will no one tell me what she sings?—
> Perhaps the plaintive numbers flow
> For old, unhappy, far-off things,
> And battles long ago;
> Or is it some more humble lay,
> Familiar matter of today?
> Some natural sorrow, loss, or pain,
> That has been, and may be again?

Whate'er the theme, the Maiden sang
As if her song could have no ending;
I saw her singing at her work,
And o'er the sickle bending—
I listened, motionless and still;
And, as I mounted up the hill,
The music in my heart I bore,
Long after it was heard no more.

1. Explain the symbolic relationship between the situation of the speaker and the Highland lass and that of the nightingale who sings to "weary bands of travellers" in the Arabian desert.
2. Explain the symbolic relationship between the nightingale and the cuckoo bird who sings "among the farthest Hebrides."
3. Explain in precise terms how the image of the singing girl leads to the speaker's conjectures about the subject of her song. (Be sure to explain why he *must* conjecture—i.e., why he doesn't understand what he hears.)

ANDREW MARVELL

THE GARDEN

How vainly men themselves amaze
To win the palm, the oak, or bays,
And their incessant labors see
Crowned from some single herb, or tree,
Whose short and narrow-vergéd shade
Does prudently their toils upbraid;
While all flowers and all trees do close
To weave the garlands of repose!

Fair Quiet, have I found thee here,
And Innocence, thy sister dear?
Mistaken long, I sought you then
In busy companies of men.
Your sacred plants, if here below,
Only among the plants will grow;
Society is all but rude
To this delicious solitude.

No white nor red was ever seen
So amorous as this lovely green.
Fond lovers, cruel as their flame,

Cut in these trees their mistress' name:
Little, alas, they know or heed
How far these beauties hers exceed!
Fair trees, wheresoe'r your barks I wound,
No name shall but your own be found.

When we have run our passion's heat,
Love hither makes his best retreat.
The gods, that mortal beauty chase,
Still in a tree did end their race:
Apollo hunted Daphne so,
Only that she might laurel grow;
And Pan did after Syrinx speed,
Not as a nymph, but for a reed.

What wondrous life is this I lead!
Ripe apples drop about my head;
The luscious clusters of the vine
Upon my mouth do crush their wine;
The nectarine and curious peach
Into my hands themselves do reach;
Stumbling on melons, as I pass,
Insnared with flowers, I fall on grass.

Meanwhile the mind, from pleasure less,
Withdraws into its happiness;
The mind, that ocean where each kind
Does straight its own resemblance find;
Yet it creates, transcending these,
Far other worlds and other seas,
Annihilating all that's made
To a green thought in a green shade.

Here at the fountain's sliding foot,
Or at some fruit tree's mossy root,
Casting the body's vest aside,
My soul into the boughs does glide:
There, like a bird, it sits and sings,
Then whets and combs its silver wings,
And, till prepared for longer flight,
Waves in its plumes the various light.

Such was that happy garden-state,
While man there walked without a mate:

After a place so pure and sweet,
What other help could yet be meet!
But 'twas beyond a mortal's share
To wander solitary there:
Two paradises 'twere in one
To live in paradise alone.

How well the skillful gardener drew
Of flowers and herbs this dial new,
Where, from above, the milder sun
Does through a fragrant zodiac run;
And as it works, th' industrious bee
Computes its time as well as we!
How could such sweet and wholesome hours
Be reckoned but with herbs and flowers?

1. Explain how the symbolic contrast between life passed amid "busy companies of men" and life passed "in paradise alone" runs through the poem.

2. How does the speaker's description of the garden relate to his image of the mind as an "ocean where each kind / Does straight its own resemblance find"?

3. Explain the symbolic meaning of the image of the soul that "into the boughs does glide" and "waves in its plumes the various light."

4. What is the relationship between the speaker's mythological allusions ("Apollo haunted Daphne so") and his biblical allusion ("that happy garden-state")? How does the biblical story of the Garden of Eden relate to the poem as a whole?

4

STRUCTURE AND THEME

When we have discovered and analyzed a pattern of symbolic meaning in a work of literature, as we did in our passage from "Ulysses," we are working at an advanced level of interpretation. We already have enough critical technique, in fact, to write a fine essay on any passage we choose: a good deal of penetrating criticism—it's called *explication*—is written at this level. But a single pattern of symbolic meaning, no matter how important it is, is still only part of a larger whole. When we take the total symbolic configuration of a work into account, we are talking about the way its images and metaphors and similes merge into a single large pattern that sustains all the others. This is the *structure* of the work.

When we talk about the structure of a work, it may sound as if we have left behind the whole idea of meaning we've talked about so far, the kind that derives from the consciousness of a single speaker and the way he views the world. This is because "structure" doesn't seem like a very appropriate term to use when we are dealing with a process of perception—it seems to go better with physical objects, like skyscrapers or geometrical constructions. But in fact that's not so: when we speak of the structure of Tennyson's "Ulysses," we are still dealing with Ulysses' perception of the world; it's just that we have stepped back far enough to view it as a whole.

When we conceive of it as a whole, a poem or a novel or a play does seem something like a fixed object, with parts that relate to other parts, elements that stand in contrast to other elements, and so on. Some writers, when trying to describe this phenomenon, invoke music as a parallel: when we hear a Beethoven symphony for the first time, we're caught up in the process of listening to each theme as it develops, each motif as it disappears and is picked up again later on. But when we have heard the same symphony a number of times, and know the score by heart, what we're aware of is the elaborate architecture of sound that embraces all those separate themes and motifs, and that makes the symphony a unified whole.

There are other analogies as well, and it doesn't matter which we invoke, as long as we realize that the concept of structure develops naturally out of the process we have been talking about all along, one that begins in a close examination of particular words and phrases, moves (through analysis of speaker, audience, and dramatic situation) to a more general level of symbolic meaning, and finally arrives at a consideration of the whole. If we say we are examining the structure of a work, we are in effect announcing that we have completed all the earlier stages in the analytic process, and that we are now ready to make some final comment about its meaning.

In the last chapter we agreed that interpretation must always, even at its most abstract level, give an account of the speaker's perception of the world, for the simple reason that a poem or a story *is* the world as it exists in the consciousness of some speaker. When we move back far enough to consider the poem or story as a whole, however, something curious happens: we begin to notice things that the speaker himself doesn't see. If we are aiming at a complete interpretation of the work, it is clear that we have to deal with this aspect of its meaning.

At first glance, this may seem to be an odd concept: how can a speaker see and not see at the same time? We might put the proposition in a slightly different way: it is perfectly possible for a speaker to see everything he describes, but to miss some or all of the significance of what he sees. Consider, for example, the case of "Haircut," a short story by Ring Lardner where a barber describes an accident he has witnessed. The barber's description is very detailed, and at a certain point we realize, even though he doesn't, that he has seen a murder. "Haircut" is an extreme example, but the story dramatizes something that happens all the time, both in life and literature, and that seems to belong to the very process of perception.

This principle underlies the concept of structure: *every literary work has a speaker who ignores some of the "objective" significance of what he sees.* This is most clear in works like "Haircut," where the narrator is so innocent or credulous that he misses the significance of almost everything he sees, but it is also true of works at the other end of the spectrum, with narrators who seem wholly conscious and entirely perceptive, and whose view of the world perhaps seems more subtle and profound than our own. This is because every speaker's vision of reality is shaped by certain attitudes that he doesn't perceive, just as a man wearing glasses does not see their lenses when he is reading a book or looking at a building. Anger, pride, disgust, sentimentality, honesty, tolerance, sensitivity—any of these may be the medium through which a speaker gazes at the world, giving a certain subjective significance to what he sees there. When we examine the structure of a poem or a story, we are really dealing with the relationship between *what* is seen and *how* it is seen—the "objective" significance of something and its significance for the speaker.

This brings us to the first of terms critics use when they're talking about literary structure: *irony*. When we use this word in everyday situations, it is usually to describe someone's attitude or tone: Oscar Wilde says somewhere that "wickedness is a myth invented by good people to account for the curious attractiveness of others"—although we see Wilde's point, which is a very witty one, we know that he is being ironic. It is perfectly proper to use the word irony in this common sense when we are describing the attitude of a speaker or a narrator, to talk about the "ironic viewpoint" of the narrator of Jane Austen's *Pride and Prejudice* or the speaker of Pope's *The Rape of the Lock.* When we use *irony* to refer to some aspect of structure, however, it is as a technical term with a very different meaning.

As a critical term, irony refers to any difference between what a speaker sees and how he sees it. So when the narrator of "Haircut" sees only an accident where there has really been a murder, we speak of this as an irony that readers have to perceive (even though the narrator doesn't) if they are to make sense of the story. Let's examine this principle in greater detail by looking at a passage from Jonathan Swift's satire *Gulliver's Travels*.

Gulliver's first voyage is to the land of Lilliput, an imaginary country where tiny people inhabit a landscape of miniature forests, fields, towns, and cities. Gulliver learns the Lilliputian language and spends some months observing their customs and government; but then trouble develops—Flimnap, the Lord High Treasurer of Lilliput and the most powerful man in its government, takes a dislike to Gulliver:

> The Treasurer took a fancy to be jealous of his wife, from the malice of some evil tongues, who informed him that her Grace had taken a violent affection for my person; and the court scandal ran for some time that she once came privately to my lodging. This I solemnly declare to be a most infamous falsehood, without any grounds . . . . I own she came often to my house, but always publicly, nor ever without three more in the coach, who were usually her sister and young daughter, and some particular acquaintance . . . . And I still appeal to my servants round, whether they at any time saw a coach at my door without knowing what persons were in it.

The joke here is obvious: Gulliver is being accused of sexual relations with a woman who is six inches tall, and the accusation is absurd not because the lady is of blameless character but because sex between them is an anatomical impossibility. This is the *what* of the situation, its objective significance. The *how* (how Gulliver perceives it) is revealed in the way Gulliver defends himself against the charge—in saying that there was always someone present when he saw the Treasurer's wife, or that his servants can vouch for the propriety of his behavior, Gulliver is reacting just as he would back in England if he had been accused of committing adultery with the wife of a friend or acquaintance. When he defends himself this way, Gulliver is showing that he does not recognize the absurdity of his situation, that he is looking at the world in an utterly naive and credulous way. The difference between Gulliver's naive perception of the situation and its actuality is what we mean by irony.

Irony in this technical sense derives wholly from the dramatic situation. Our ordinary use of the term asks us to look for someone who is *being* ironic, and this is never the case when we speak of irony as an aspect of literary structure. If we were to show this passage from *Gulliver's Travels* to someone who didn't know anything about literary criticism, it is true that he might read it and declare that "Swift is being ironic," but it would take us only a few moments to demonstrate that this is not so, that Gulliver (not Swift) is telling the story, that Gulliver himself gives us all the information necessary to understand the "objective" situation—i.e., that he is normal human size, the Treasurer's wife a miniature woman—and that the irony is something that develops from the disparity between the objective situation and the way Gulliver perceives it.

Now let's look at another term critics use when they're dealing with this sort of situation: *tension*. It gets pretty awkward after a while to have to keep talking about "the difference between what Gulliver actually sees and how he sees it"—it is much more economical simply to say that there is a tension between the two. When we use the term tension to describe what is going on, however, we are doing much more than noting that there is a difference: we are recognizing that our "objective" view of the situation and Gulliver's view are alternative versions of the same reality, that the two views are interdependent (that is, neither could exist without the other), and that irony is something that runs through the work as a whole. When we are reading *Gulliver's Travels*, there is a continuous interaction between our perception of events and Gulliver's, and through this we eventually come to understand the symbolic meaning of the story.

This returns us to the concept of symbolic structure, for irony and tension are not just things we observe in particular scenes or episodes, but principles that give shape to the work as a whole. All through *Gulliver's Travels* we have to deal with the relationship between what Gulliver actually sees and the way he sees it, the real significance of his adventures and his naive perception of them. This is why, when we step back and view *Gulliver's Travels* as a whole, it begins to look something like a fixed object: the reason we can talk about how parts of Gulliver's story relate to other parts is that a certain underlying tension runs through them all, contributing an eventual unity of meaning.

I have already mentioned Ernst Cassirer's description of the literary work as "a self-contained cosmos with its own center of gravity." When we are considering irony and tension as principles of literary structure, this is a particularly appropriate metaphor: gravity operates in the universe as a force that holds things in fixed relationships, preventing a collapse into chaotic diversity. When we speak of the "world" of *Gulliver's Travels* or *Paradise Lost* or *King Lear*, we are talking about these works as symbolic wholes in which irony and tension operate as laws of unity, drawing a complex variety of themes and episodes and symbolic motifs into one large comprehensible order.

The concept of symbolic structure takes on its full meaning only when we are considering some literary work as a whole, so let's apply what we know about tension and irony to Keats's sonnet "Bright Star." This time, let us assume the preliminary stages of critical analysis and begin at the level of symbolic meaning:

> Bright star, would I were steadfast as thou art—
> Not in lone splendor hung aloft the night
> And watching, with eternal lids apart,
> Like nature's patient, sleepless Eremite,
> The moving waters at their priestlike task   5
> Of pure ablution round earth's human shores,
> Or gazing on the new soft fallen mask
> Of snow upon the mountains and the moors—
> No—yet still steadfast, still unchangeable,
> Pillow'd upon my fair love's ripening breast,   10
> To feel forever its soft fall and swell,
> Awake for ever in a sweet unrest,
> Still, still to hear her tender-taken breath,
> And so live ever—or else swoon to death.

When we look at the sonnet as a symbolic whole, the first thing we are likely to notice is that there is a contrast between the first part of the poem and the second. Lines 1–8 describe not only the bright star *in lone splendor hung aloft the night,* but (by implication) the entire physical universe as it exists apart from human life and passion.

This is an idea that occurs frequently in literature, for in contemplating the stars we are contemplating Nature in her remote and unchanging aspect, as something infinitely greater than, and oblivious to, the state of man.

Then, in lines 9–14, we have a scene that belongs very much to the realm of human life and passion: the picture of two lovers in bed together, the speaker pillowed upon his fair love's ripening breast, intensely aware of her physical presence and the small natural movements of her body. The important thing about this scene, though, is not simply that it pictures a human situation, but that it does so in a way that emphasizes the mutability (change, growth, death, decay) of human life. We shall see why this is so later on; for the moment, let's assume that Keats's picture of the two lovers is something like the scene Yeats describes in a poem called "Sailing to Byzantium"—

> The young
> In one another's arms, birds in the trees
> —Those dying generations—at their song . . . .

—and that the major contrast in the sonnet is between the star (eternal, unchanging) and the lovers (human, mutable).

Some critics, if they were asked to describe the structure of "Bright Star," would say that this contrast is the "central structural device" of the poem. This is one way of describing the larger symbolic unity of the sonnet, but it is perhaps best to avoid the word "device" as it is used in this context: it not only sounds awkward, but it seems to refer to what someone thinks Keats was doing when he wrote the poem, not to the consciousness of the speaker inside the poem. Instead of simply observing that there is this symbolic contrast in "Bright Star," then, let us concentrate on the speaker's view of experience and see if we can discover why the contrast occurs in the first place.

When we looked at our passage from *Gulliver's Travels*, we observed that there was a distinct limitation to Gulliver's view of events, and that we continuously had to account for the difference between their "objective" significance and their significance for Gulliver; this difference we described by the term irony. When we turn to "Bright Star," it appears as though we are dealing with an entirely different sort of work—a short poem rather than a long prose narrative, a meditative sonnet instead of a satire—but we also know there are certain basic similarities: speaker, dramatic audience, etc. So let's begin by seeing how the principle of irony, which derives from those basic similarities, operates here. Consider, once again, the speaker's description of the star he is contemplating:

> Not in lone splendor hung aloft the night
> And watching, with eternal lids apart,
> Like nature's patient, sleepless Eremite . . . .

Here, we find that we are dealing once again with metaphor. When the speaker says that the star is *watching*, it means that he is perceiving the star as something endowed with human consciousness; when he describes it as having its *eternal lids apart*, the star becomes (metaphorically) the eye of some cosmic observer. Then, when he describes the star as *nature's patient, sleepless Eremite*, we discover more precisely how he conceives of this cosmic observer: as a devout hermit who lives in isolation out of a desire to worship nature, just as religious hermits retire to the mountains or the desert to live in pure contemplation of God.

As we listen to the speaker addressing the star in its lonely splendor, however, our minds are simultaneously occupied with a more normal version of things—that is, we are aware that stars are not eyes but bodies composed of atoms and electrons, and that they are not conscious but simply exist as phenomena of the physical universe. All this belongs to what we know about the "objective" significance of what the speaker is seeing, but since his metaphors seem to insist on a quite different perception of the same reality, we know that we have once again come across the principle of irony.

And at the same time, the principle of tension. We have defined tension as the interaction between our view of events and the speaker's view. When the speaker describes the star as a *sleepless Eremite*, he is simultaneously affirming our version of things and his own. We know that stars are sleepless because physical bodies don't sleep—that's something only living things can do, and it makes no more sense to talk about stars sleeping than it does to talk about rocks or sticks of wood sleeping. But for the speaker, who perceives the star as a kind of solitary hermit of the skies, its sleeplessness represents a conscious state, like the lonely nighttime watch of the religious hermit living in a cave. This is what we mean when we say that tension is a structural (or ordering) principle: the phrase *sleepless Eremite* keeps both the "objective" significance of things and the speaker's perception of them in view, and creates out of a simple irony ("I see this star as a hermit") a symbolic movement that draws together the various elements of the poem.

If we assume an analysis of the way in which this symbolic movement continues through the next few lines of the poem (note how *priestlike* and *ablution* develop the religious metaphor introduced with *Eremite*), we can look ahead to the last six lines:

> No—and yet still steadfast, still unchangeable,
>   Pillow'd upon my fair love's ripening breast,
> To feel for ever its soft fall and swell,
>   Awake for ever in a sweet unrest,
> Still, still to hear her tender-taken breath,
> And so live ever—or else swoon to death.

This, we agreed, is the human situation that stands in contrast to the star in its lonely splendor. But now that we have looked more closely at the irony implicit in the speaker's perception of the star, let us see if we can discover the unity within the contrast.

Of all the words the speaker used to describe the star in the earlier part of the poem, the one that best fits our normal view of the heavens is *eternal*. Of course, the speaker doesn't say anything like "The stars remain the same while generations of men grow old and die": he simply shows that he recognizes the star as something fixed and unchanging. But even while he talks about the star as an eternal object, we've seen, he is perceiving it as something that has human qualities like consciousness, vigilance, and patience.

When we come to the speaker's description of himself and his lover in bed, we seem to be in a situation far removed from the star in its remote watchfulness. We have, first of all, not just an idea of sexual love but an idea of human companionship: two lovers together, in contrast to the star in its lone splendor. Then we are aware that the lovers, as human beings, are subject to the natural cycle of growth and decay: when the speaker describes himself as being pillowed upon his love's ripening breast, for instance, we have come upon a new kind of irony: *ripening* is a word that is normally used to describe things that grow in the earth (wheat or corn or melons) and that come and go with the seasons.

Yet there are signs that the way the speaker perceives this human situation is really not so different from the way he viewed the star. When he speaks of the *soft fall and swell* of his lover's breast, he seems to be describing something like the movement of the ocean, something belonging to the eternal rhythms of nature. And although he does not use the word eternal when he is describing this scene, his phrases reveal that he is viewing it in some such light: *forever, still* (which here means "always"), *and so live ever*, etc.

We do not need to do a full interpretation of "Bright Star" to see the basic point: the *nature* that encompasses the star and the lovers is one and the same, and in identifying imaginatively with nature one participates in eternity while retaining human consciousness. The important thing to observe is the way irony and tension—the continuous interaction between our "objective" view of things and the speaker's metaphoric view—operate as principles that shape the poem. While the speaker's perception of the star endows it with certain human qualities, his perception of himself and his lover endows them with qualities belonging to the star, and the poem as a whole moves toward a vision where these differences dissolve in a larger imaginative unity. This is a unity we glimpse only when we allow our awareness of the structure of "Bright Star" to guide our interpretation of its meaning.

We must now consider one of the most important technical terms critics use when they are doing interpretation—*theme*. When we were discussing a passage from Tennyson's "Ulysses" in the last chapter, we discovered that Ulysses uses a number of metaphors that involve roughly the same idea: "experience is the sustenance of the spirit." At the time, we called this a symbolic pattern, but in fact it is more normally referred to as a theme.

When we talk about the theme of a literary work, we are coming at the work from a slightly different angle than before: a theme is not a symbolic pattern merely, but *a symbolic pattern isolated for critical discussion*. In using the term, we are in effect announcing that we have performed what is called an abstractive act—that is, we are simplifying, for purposes of interpretation, something we actually recognize as having a complex relationship to all the other elements of a symbolic structure.

This act of simplification does not mean that we are trying to make the work any simpler than it really is. Abstractive description is something literary criticism shares with many other disciplines, and its purpose is always to lead back to an awareness of complexity and coherence. The historian who describes the railroads of Victorian England, the physiologist who explains the human respiratory system, the critic who discusses the theme of demonic parody in *Paradise Lost,* are all ultimately concerned with a totality that lies beyond abstraction —with all of Victorian England, with the human body as an entire physiological system, with *Paradise Lost* as a whole.

When we talk about theme in shorter works—"the theme of Keats's 'Bright Star' concerns escape from mutability through imaginative identification with nature"—we are sometimes very close to what the naive reader of literature calls the "moral" or "message" of the work. This is to ignore the abstractive nature of thematic interpretation, and to mistake the nature of literature itself. As we have seen all along, poems and novels and plays don't have morals or messages: they simply show us a certain dramatic situation and leave us to draw our own conclusions. The sonnet "Bright Star" does not command anyone to go out and contemplate the heavens in an attempt to escape his sense of frail mortality, nor does it even suggest that this is a wise thing to do: it simply presents the notion of such escape as an imaginative possibility and leaves the reader to consider it on his own.

In longer works, the danger is that we shall confuse theme with subject. We are on perfectly legitimate ground, for instance, when we choose to discuss "the theme of marriage" in Jane Austen's *Pride and Prejudice,* but by this we must mean more than that the subject of marriage comes up a lot in the novel. Theme, once again, is a *symbolic pattern* isolated for critical discussion: when we notice that marriage appears in the story both as a symbol of spiritual imprisonment (when people marry for the wrong reasons) and a symbol of spiritual union (when they marry for the right ones), we are legitimately dealing with marriage as a theme. To interpret the theme, of course, we must deal with the larger question of what makes the right reasons right and the wrong reasons wrong, but that is precisely what our prior analysis of narrator, dramatic situation, tone, and symbolic structure will have prepared us to do.

In any event, the relation of theme to subject is variable. To see how we manage the concept of theme when writing about literature, let's look at some episodes from Alexander Pope's mock-epic poem *The Rape of the Lock.* The plot of the poem is simple: a beautiful young lady has a dream about an unrevealed "dread event," wakes up and is dressed by her maid, goes on a river outing with other young people, and during the outing has a lock of her hair cut off by an amorous young nobleman. But the poem itself is brilliant and complex, describing trivial events in the elevated style we associate with epics like the *Iliad* or the *Aeneid,* and parodying the seriousness with which people view their everyday concerns.

Let us begin with a passage from Canto II, where Belinda, the young heroine of the poem, is being dressed by her maid. In the previous Canto, we have learned that young virgins like Belinda are guarded by invisible creatures called Sylphs; Belinda is surrounded by an entire army of them, and in this episode their chief, Ariel, is giving them their assignments:

> To fifty chosen Sylphs, of special note,
> We trust th'important charge, the petticoat:
> Oft have we known that sevenfold fence to fail,
> Tho' stiff with hoops, and armed with ribs of whale.
> Form a strong line about the silver bound,
> And guard the wide circumference around.

Here, once again, we run into the familiar principles of irony and tension: in describing Belinda's petticoat (a wide one, with hoops, as worn by women in the eighteenth century) in the terms he does (*sevenfold fence, armed with ribs of whale*), Ariel shows that he is viewing the trivial business of a young lady's dressing as an epic event. But beneath the comedy there is a serious point: Belinda's petticoat is being described as though it were part of the armor of an epic hero, and the idea of armor involves the idea of war. When a hero's shield "fails" him in an epic poem, we know what it means: a spear or an arrow has pierced through and wounded him. But what kind of war does a young woman fight in, and how can her petticoat "fail" as armor? Let's keep that question in mind as we look at another scene, this time in Canto III. We are now out on the Thames, and Belinda has begun a game of cards with the young lord who admires her:

> The skillful Nymph reviews her force with care;
> *Let spades be trumps!* she said, and trumps they were.
> Now move to war her sable Matadores,
> In show like leaders of the swarthy Moors.
> Spadillo first, unconquerable lord!
> Led off two captive trumps, and swept the board.

Once again, we have an ordinary event being described in terms of war. The important thing seems to be not simply that a card game can be described as a battle, where such terms as *force* and *leaders* and *captive* are appropriate to the symbolic action, but that it is Belinda's situation—playing against a man, and specifically against the young Baron who will later cut off a lock of her hair—which makes the terms appropriate. Now let us look ahead to Canto V; the Baron has cut off Belinda's lock, and she is outraged. The other women take her side, and the ensuing scene is one of open hostility:

> While through the press enraged Thalestris flies,
> And scatters deaths around from both her eyes,
> A beau and witling perished in the throng,
> One died in metaphor, and one in song.
> *O cruel Nymph! a living death I bear,*
> Cried Dapperwit, and sunk beside his chair.
> A mournful glance Sir Fopling upwards cast,
> *Those eyes are made so killing*—was his last.

All that is being described here is a "war" of looks and reproaches, where the women who have adopted Belinda's cause turn their anger on the men who stood by and let the incident happen. But in a poem where so many other things have been described in the language of battle, the episode seems to be some sort of symbolic culmination.

If we were to deal with these passages in an essay on *The Rape of the Lock*, we would say that we were going to discuss "the battle of the sexes" as a major theme of the poem. In this case, notice how many different subjects the concept of theme embraces: description of a young lady's petticoat, of a card game, of an unpleasant social incident, and much more. What seems to draw all these various subjects into the same *symbolic* focus is an idea of the necessary antagonism that exists between men and women, even in a very civilized society.

4. STRUCTURE AND THEME

This is a serious subject, and to explore it at any great length we would have to spend more time than we have examining the symbolic structure of *The Rape of the Lock*. But the basic idea is clear enough: the antagonism is, on one level, sexual—the women in the poem are expected by society to guard their virginity, and the men regard their virginity as something to be conquered (that is how Belinda's petticoat would "fail" as armor). On a more abstract level, the antagonism is psychological: a beautiful young woman like Belinda, surrounded by lovers, is in a dominant and independent position, but one that involves an unhappy paradox—if she marries someone attracted by her youth and beauty, she will lose her independence, but if to preserve her independence she delays getting married, she will lose her youth and beauty and the men they attract. On both levels, the relationship of men and women in the poem is morally ambivalent, and this ambivalence is the source of the theme of symbolic battle.

The concept of theme implies an entire mode of interpretation, the most advanced we shall consider in this book. As we shall see in the next two chapters, the general method of analysis and interpretation we have learned through reading poetry is also employed, with some minor variations, in reading and writing about fiction and drama. Our brief discussion of *The Rape of Lock*, however, will have suggested why thematic interpretation occupies, on every level from the college classroom to the pages of learned journals, the center of modern literary study: it provides not only a way of reading literature— any sort of reading might do that—but of perceiving literary meaning in its own terms.

This is the ultimate aim of literary study. In discussing method in these chapters we have focused on a mode of comprehension that begins in something close to ordinary reading and ends in the interpretation of symbolic meaning. Yet when our general method of analysis and interpretation is mastered through practice, it soon ceases to appear in the light of "a method"—it becomes a new way of reading, as easy and familiar as ordinary reading but with a much greater scope of comprehension. This is in turn the aim of interpretation: when we elucidate thematic meaning in poems and novels and plays, we are demonstrating that we have learned to move freely in imagined worlds existing alternatively to our own.

ANALYSIS AND INTERPRETATION

The first three selections in this section are poems entire in themselves, and you are asked to analyze their symbolic structure in the same manner as in our discussion of "Bright Star." Try to keep in mind the relation of each image, metaphor, and simile to the meaning of the poem as a whole, and to derive from your analysis a total explanation of the speaker's perception of the world. When dealing with patterns of symbolic meaning within the poem, account for any difference between the "objective" state of affairs described and their significance for the speaker.

The next five selections in the section are provided as exercises in thematic analysis, and your answers to the questions following the selections may be taken as raw material for a medium-length (3–4 page) critical essay on theme in one or more of the selections.

W. B. YEATS

THE ROSE OF THE WORLD

Who dreamed that beauty passes like a dream?
For these red lips, with all their mournful pride,
Mournful that no new wonder may betide,
Troy passed away in one high funeral gleam,
And Usna's children died.   5

We and the laboring world are passing by:
Amid men's souls, that waver and give place
Like the pale waters in their wintry race,
Under the passing stars, foam of the sky,
Lives on this lonely face.   10

Bow down, archangels, in your dim abode:
Before you were, or any hearts to beat,
Weary and kind one lingered by His seat;
He made the world to be a grassy road
Before her wandering feet.

1. The "red lips," "lonely face," and "wandering feet" mentioned by the speaker belong to a single female figure, yet he implies that she is *both* Helen of Troy and the beautiful Deirdre of the Irish legend. Explain this paradox, and show how it is central to the symbolic structure of the poem.

2. Look up and give an account of the Irish myth to which the phrase "Usna's children" refers us. How is it parallel to the story of the Trojan War as we find it in Homer and elsewhere? In what precise sense do the parallels define "the rose of the world" as the speaker conceives of her? How does myth function symbolically in the poem as a whole (note the mythic dimension of lines 11–14)?

3. What is the symbolic significance of these phrases in lines 6–9: *laboring world; passing by; waver and give place; passing stars; foam of the sky*? How do the ideas of permanence and change (or immortality and mortality) relate this stanza to stanzas 1 and 3? How does this relationship illuminate the symbolic structure of the poem as a whole?

LANGSTON HUGHES

THEME FOR ENGLISH B

The instructor said,

> *Go home and write*
> *a page tonight.*
> *And let that page come out of you—*
> *Then, it will be true.*　　　　　　　　　　　　　　5

I wonder if it's that simple?
I am twenty-two, colored, born in Winston-Salem.
I went to school there, then Durham, then here
to this college on the hill above Harlem.
I am the only colored student in my class.　　　　　10
The steps from the hill lead down into Harlem,
through a park, then I cross St. Nicholas,
Eighth Avenue, Seventh, and I come to the Y,
the Harlem Branch Y, where I take the elevator
up to my room, sit down, and write this page:　　　15

It's not easy to know what is true for you or me
at twenty-two, my age. But I guess I'm what
I feel and see and hear, Harlem, I hear you:
hear you, hear me—we two—you, me, talk on this page.
(I hear New York, too.) Me—who?　　　　　　　　20

Well, I like to eat, sleep, drink, and be in love.
I like to work, read, learn, and understand life.
I like a pipe for a Christmas present,
or records—Bessie, bop, or Bach.
I guess being colored doesn't make me *not* like　　25
the same things other folks like who are other races.
So will my page be colored that I write?

Being me, it will not be white.
But it will be
a part of you, instructor.   30
You are white—
yet a part of me, as I am a part of you.
That's American.
Sometimes perhaps you don't want to be a part of me.
Nor do I often want to be a part of you.   35
But we are, that's true!
As I learn from you,
I guess you learn from me—
although you're older—and white—
and somewhat more free.   40

This is my page for English B.

1. What elements in the poem suggest that it is a response to a class assignment ("*go home and write / a page tonight*")? What elements suggest that it is a personal meditation? How are these related within the total structure of the poem?

2. What is the precise symbolic relationship of lines 8–15 to lines 21–27? of lines 1–5 to lines 28–40? (Note that lines 1–5, and not lines 28–40, define the dramatic audience.) What do your conclusions suggest about symbolic structure?

3. What do the following phrases suggest about the symbolic meaning of the poem: *Harlem, I hear you; Bessie, bop, or Bach; will my page be colored; that's American; somewhat more free*? How does the phrase *we two—you, me, talk on this page* help define the tone of the poem? How does tone relate to structure and meaning here?

JOHN DONNE

AIR AND ANGELS

> Twice or thrice had I loved thee,
> Before I knew thy face or name;
> So in a voice, so in a shapeless flame,
> Angels affect us oft, and worshipped be;
>   Still when, to where thou wert, I came,   5
> Some lovely glorious nothing I did see.
>   But since my soul, whose child love is,
> Takes limbs of flesh, and else could nothing do,
>   More subtle than the parent is
> Love must not be, but take a body too;   10

And therefore what thou wert, and who,
  I bid love ask, and now
That it assume thy body I allow,
And fix itself in thy lip, eye, and brow.

Whilst thus to ballast love I thought,   15
And so more steadily to have gone,
With wares which would sink admiration,
I saw I had love's pinnace overfraught;
  Every thy hair for love to work upon
Is much too much, some fitter must be sought;   20
  For, nor in nothing, nor in things
Extreme and scatt'ring bright, can love inhere.
  Then as an angel, face and wings
Of air, not pure as it, yet pure doth wear,
  So thy love may be my love's sphere.   25
  Just such disparity
As is 'twixt air and angels' purity,
'Twixt women's love and men's will ever be.

    1. How does the difference " 'twixt air and angels' purity" sym-
bolically inform the speaker's description of his love affair in the first
stanza?

    2. How does the speaker's description of love as a "pinnace" re-
late to his argument about the difference between men's and women's
love? What is actually being described in lines 15–18?

    3. What is the exact symbolic relationship, as the speaker de-
scribes it, between a man's love of a woman and a mortal's worship of
an angel? How does the idea of worship operate in the poem as a
whole?

ROBERT BROWNING

MY LAST DUCHESS

That's my last Duchess painted on the wall,
Looking as if she were alive. I call
That piece a wonder, now: Frà Pandolf's hands
Worked busily a day, and there she stands.
Will't please you sit and look at her? I said   5
"Frà Pandolf" by design, for never read
Strangers like you that pictured countenance,
The depth and passion of its earnest glance,
But to myself they turned (since none puts by

The curtain I have drawn for you, but I)   10
And seemed as they would ask me, if they durst,
How such a glance came there; so, not the first
Are you to turn and ask thus. Sir, 'twas not
Her husband's presence only, called that spot
Of joy into the Duchess' cheek: perhaps   15
Frà Pandolf chanced to say "Her mantle laps
Over my lady's wrist too much," or "Paint
Must never hope to reproduce the faint
Half-flush that dies along her throat": such stuff
Was courtesy, she thought, and cause enough   20
For calling up that spot of joy. She had
A heart—how shall I say?—too soon made glad,
Too easily impressed; she liked whate'er
She looked on, and her looks went everywhere.
Sir, 'twas all one! My favor at her breast,   25
The dropping of the daylight in the West,
The bough of cherries some officious fool
Broke in the orchard for her, the white mule
She rode with round the terrace—all and each
Would draw from her alike the approving speech,   30
Or blush, at least. She thanked men—good! but thanked
Somehow—I know not how—as if she ranked
My gift of a nine-hundred-years-old name
With anybody's gift. Who'd stoop to blame
This sort of trifling? Even had you skill   35
In speech—(which I have not)—to make your will
Quite clear to such an one, and say, "Just this
Or that in you disgusts me; here you miss,
Or there exceed the mark"—and if she let
Herself be lessoned so, nor plainly set   40
Her wits to yours, forsooth, and made excuse
—E'en then would be some stooping; and I choose
Never to stoop. Oh sir, she smiled, no doubt,
Whene'er I passed her; but who passed without
Much the same smile? This grew; I gave commands;   45
Then all smiles stopped together. There she stands
As if alive. Will't please you rise? We'll meet
The company below. then. I repeat,
The Count your master's known munificence
Is ample warrant that no just pretense   50

Of mine for dowry will be disallowed;
Though his fair daughter's self, as I avowed
At starting, is my object. Nay, we'll go
Together down, sir. Notice Neptune, though,
Taming a sea horse, thought a rarity,   55
Which Claus of Innsbruck cast in bronze for me!

1. Who is speaking? To whom is he speaking? What is the purpose of their conversation? How do we know that this monologue represents a long digression from the subject at hand? Is it really a digression?

2. What is the speaker's relation to the "pictured countenance" (*not* to the actual woman represented)? How does he expect his audience to react to his speech? How does his language reveal this expectation?

3. What do the following phrases tell us about the speaker's perception of himself and his deceased wife: *calling up that spot of joy; draw from her alike the approving speech, or blush; stoop to blame; all smiles stopped?*

4. Why does the speaker pause to discuss this portrait? In what sense is his commentary on the portrait a conscious commentary on his own personality? What is the symbolic significance of the portrait?

CHARLES DICKENS

From *LITTLE DORRIT*, Chapter I

Thirty years ago, Marseilles lay burning in the sun, one day. A blazing sun upon a fierce August day was no greater rarity in southern France then, than at any other time, before or since. Everything in Marseilles, and about Marseilles, had stared at the fervid sky, and been stared at in return, until a staring habit had become universal there. Strangers were stared out of countenance by staring white houses, staring white walls, staring white streets, staring tracts of arid road, staring hills from which verdure was burnt away. The only things to be seen not fixed staring and glaring were the vines drooping under their load of grapes. These did occasionally wink a little, as the hot air barely moved their leaves.

There was no wind to make a ripple on the foul water within the harbour, or on the beautiful sea without. The line of demarcation between the two colours, black and blue, showed the point which the pure sea would not pass; but it lay as quiet as the abominable pool, with which it never mixed. Boats without awnings were too hot to touch; ships blistered at their moorings; the stones of the quays had not cooled, night or day, for months. Hindoos, Russians, Chinese, Spaniards, Portuguese, Englishmen, Frenchmen, Genoese, Neapolitans, Venetians, Greeks, Turks, descendants from all the builders of Babel, come to trade at Marseilles, sought the shade alike—taking refuge in any hiding-place from a sea too intensely blue to be looked at, and a sky of purple, set with one great flaming jewel of fire.

The universal stare made the eyes ache. Towards the distant line of Italian coast, indeed, it was a little relieved by light clouds of mist, slowly rising from the evaporation of the sea, but it softened nowhere else. Far away the staring roads, deep in dust, stared from the hill-side, stared from the hollow, stared from the interminable plain. Far away the dusty vines overhanging wayside cottages, and the monotonous wayside avenues of parched trees without shade, drooped beneath the stare of earth and sky. So did the horses with drowsy bells, in long lines of carts, creeping slowly towards the interior; so did their recumbent drivers, when they were awake, which rarely happened; so did the exhausted labourers in the fields. Everything that lived or grew, was oppressed by the glare; except the lizard, passing swiftly over rough stone walls, and the cicada, chirping his dry hot chirp, like a rattle. The very dust was scorched brown, and something quivered in the atmosphere as if the air itself were panting.

Blinds, shutters, curtains, awnings, were all closed and drawn to keep out the stare. Grant it but a chink or keyhole, and it shot in like a white-hot arrow. The churches were the freest from it. To come out of the twilight of pillars and arches—dreamily dotted with winking lamps, dreamily peopled with ugly old shadows piously dozing, spitting, and begging—was to plunge into a fiery river, and swim for life to the nearest strip of shade. So, with people lounging and lying wherever shade was, with but little hum of tongues or barking of dogs, with occasional jangling of discordant church bells and rattling of vicious drums, Marseilles, a fact to be strongly smelt and tasted, lay broiling in the sun one day.

In Marseilles that day there was a villainous prison. In one of its chambers, so repulsive a place that even the obtrusive stare blinked at it, and left it such refuse of reflected light as it could find for itself, were two men. Besides the two men, a notched and disfigured bench, immovable from the wall, with a draught-board rudely hacked upon it with a knife, a set of draughts, made of old buttons and soup bones, a set of dominoes, two mats, and two or three wine bottles. That was all the chamber held, exclusive of rats and other unseen vermin, in addition to the seen vermin, the two men.

It received such light as it got through a grating of iron bars fashioned like a pretty large window, by means of which it could be always inspected from the gloomy staircase on which the grating gave. There was a broad strong ledge of stone to this grating where the bottom of it was let into the masonry, three or four feet above the ground. Upon it, one of the two men lolled half sitting and half lying, with his knees drawn up, and his feet and shoulders planted against the opposite sides of the aperture. The bars were wide enough apart to admit of his thrusting his arm through to the elbow; and so he held on negligently, for his greater ease.

A prison taint was on everything here. The imprisoned air, the imprisoned light, the imprisoned damps, the imprisoned men, were all deteriorated by confinement. As the captive men were faded and haggard, so the iron was rusty, the stone was slimy, the wood was rotten, the air was faint, the light was dim. Like a well, like a vault, like a tomb, the prison had no knowledge of the brightness outside, and would have kept its polluted atmosphere intact in one of the spice islands of the Indian Ocean.

1. Describe the relationship between narrator and dramatic audience. What is the narrator's attitude toward Marseilles? toward the prison? toward the inmates? To what degree is the dramatic audience expected to share these attitudes?

2. What do the following phrases tell us about the narrator's perception of the world: *lay burning in the sun; stared at the fervid sky; staring white houses, staring white walls* (etc.); *all the builders of Babel; one great flaming jewel of fire; like a white-hot arrow; horses with drowsy bells; jangling of discordant church bells and rattling of vicious drums; plunge into a fiery river; the imprisoned air, the imprisoned men; the prison had no knowledge of the brightness?*

3. What is the symbolic significance of the contrast between the world outside the prison and the world within the prison? How does this significance derive from the narrator's perception of the scenes he is describing? How might we analyze the contrast in thematic terms? What interpretation of the scene does this analysis suggest?

ALFRED, LORD TENNYSON
From *IDYLLS OF THE KING*

> Then saw they how there hove a dusky barge,
> Dark as a funeral scarf from stem to stern,
> Beneath them; and descending they were ware

That all the decks were dense with stately forms,
Black-stoled, black-hooded, like a dream—by these   365
Three Queens with crowns of gold: and from them rose
A cry that shivered to the tingling stars,
And, as it were one voice, an agony
Of lamentation, like a wind that shrills
All night in a waste land, where no one comes,   370
Or hath come, since the making of the world.

Then murmured Arthur, "Place me in the barge."
So to the barge they came. There those three Queens
Put forth their hands, and took the king, and wept.
But she, that rose the tallest of them all   375
And fairest, laid his head upon her lap,
And loosed the shattered casque, and chafed his hands,
And called him by his name, complaining loud,
And dropping bitter tears against a brow
Striped with dark blood: for all his face was white   380
And colorless, and like the withered moon
Smote by the fresh beam of the springing east;
And all his greaves and cuisses dashed with drops
Of onset; and the light and lustrous curls—
That made his forehead like a rising sun   385
High from the daïs-throne—were parched with dust;
Or, clotted into points and hanging loose,
Mixed with the knightly growth that fringed his lips.
So like a shattered column lay the King;
Not like that Arthur who, with lance in rest,   390
From spur to plume a star of tournament,
Shot through the lists at Camelot, and charged
Before the eyes of ladies and of kings.

Then loudly cried the bold Sir Bedivere:
"Ah! my Lord Arthur, whither shall I go?   395
Where shall I hide my forehead and my eyes?
For now I see the true old times are dead,
When every morning brought a noble chance,
And every chance brought out a noble knight.
Such times have been not since the light that led   400
The holy Elders with the gift of myrrh.
But now the whole Round Table is dissolved
Which was an image of the mighty world,
And I, the last, go forth companionless,

And the days darken round me, and the years,   405
Among new men, strange faces, other minds."

  And slowly answered Arthur from the barge:
"The old order changeth, yielding place to new,
And God fulfills himself in many ways,
Lest one good custom should corrupt the world.   410
Comfort thyself: what comfort is in me?
I have lived my life, and that which I have done
May He within himself make pure! but thou,
If thou shouldst never see my face again,
Pray for my soul. More things are wrought by prayer   415
Than this world dreams of. Wherefore, let thy voice
Rise like a fountain for me night and day.
For what are men better than sheep or goats
That nourish a blind life within the brain,
If, knowing God, they lift not hands of prayer   420
Both for themselves and those who call them friend?
For so the whole round earth is every way
Bound by gold chains about the feet of God.
But now farewell. I am going a long way
With these thou seest—if indeed I go—   425
(For all my mind is clouded with a doubt)—
To the island-valley of Avilion;
Where falls not hail, or rain, or any snow,
Nor ever wind blows loudly; but it lies
Deep-meadowed, happy, fair with orchard lawns   430
And bowery hollows crowned with summer sea,
Where I will heal me of my grievous wound."

  So said he, and the barge with oar and sail
Moved from the brink, like some full-breasted swan
That, fluting a wild carol ere her death,   435
Ruffles her pure cold plume, and takes the flood
With swarthy webs. Long stood Sir Bedivere
Revolving many memories, till the hull
Looked one black dot against the verge of dawn,
And on the mere the wailing died away.   440

    1. Describe the narrator's attitude toward the events he is describing. Does he conceive of his audience as being already familiar with the story he is telling? How does he conceive of their attitude toward these scenes?

2. What do the following phrases suggest about the narrator's perception of the world he is describing: *the decks were dense with stately forms* (364); *black-stoled, black-hooded, like a dream* (365); *shivered to the tingling stars* (367); *a wind that shrills / All night in a waste land, where no one comes* (369–370); *white / And colorless, and like the withered moon* (380–381); *so like a shattered column lay the King* (389); *like some full-breasted swan / . . . fluting a wild carol ere her death* (434–435)?

3. What do the following phrases suggest about King Arthur's perception of the same world: *a blind life within the brain* (419); *bound by gold chains about the feet of God* (423); *deep-meadowed, happy, fair with orchard lawns / And bowery hollows crowned with summer sea* (430–431)?

4. What do the following phrases suggest about Sir Bedivere's perception of the scene: *the true old times are dead* (397); *the whole Round Table is dissolved / Which was an image of the mighty world* (402–403); *new men, strange faces, other minds* (406)?

5. What is the symbolic relationship between the narrator's perception of these scenes and King Arthur's? between Arthur's and Sir Bedivere's? between Sir Bedivere's and the narrator's? What is the thematic significance of these relationships? What interpretation of the scene to they suggest?

6. Compare these scenes from *Idylls of the King* to the parallel episode from Malory's *Morte Darthur* on pages 61–62. Is simultaneous thematic interpretation of both passages possible? why? What kind of *critical* perspective is suggested by the comparison?

W. B. YEATS

EASTER 1916

> I have met them at close of day
> Coming with vivid faces
> From counter or desk among grey
> Eighteenth-century houses.
> I have passed with a nod of the head   5
> Or polite meaningless words,
> Or have lingered awhile and said
> Polite meaningless words,
> And thought before I had done
> Of a mocking tale or a gibe   10
> To please a companion
> Around the fire at the club,
> Being certain that they and I

But lived where motley is worn:
All changed, changed utterly: 15
A terrible beauty is born.

That woman's days were spent
In ignorant good-will,
Her nights in argument
Until her voice grew shrill.   20
What voice more sweet than hers
When, young and beautiful,
She rode to harriers?
This man had kept a school
And rode our winged horse;   25
This other his helper and friend
Was coming into his force;
He might have won fame in the end,
So sensitive his nature seemed,
So daring and sweet his thought.   30
This other man I had dreamed
A drunken, vainglorious lout.
He had done most bitter wrong
To some who are near my heart,
Yet I number him in the song;   35
He, too, has resigned his part
In the casual comedy;
He, too, has been changed in his turn,
Transformed utterly:
A terrible beauty is born.   40

Hearts with one purpose alone
Through summer and winter seem
Enchanted to a stone
To trouble the living stream.
The horse that comes from the road,   45
The rider, the birds that range
From cloud to tumbling cloud
Minute by minute they change;
A shadow of cloud on the stream
Changes minute by minute;   50
A horse-hoof slides on the brim,
And a horse plashes within it;
The long-legged moor-hens dive,
And hens to moor-cocks call;

Minute by minute they live: 55
The stone's in the midst of all.

Too long a sacrifice
Can make a stone of the heart.
O when may it suffice?
That is Heaven's part, our part   60
To murmur name upon name,
As a mother names her child
When sleep at last has come
On limbs that had run wild.
What is it but nightfall?   65
No, no, not night but death;
Was it needless death after all?
For England may keep faith
For all that is done and said.
We know their dream; enough   70
To know they dreamed and are dead;
And what if excess of love
Bewildered them till they died?
I write it out in a verse—
MacDonagh and MacBride   75
And Connolly and Pearse
Now and in time to be,
Wherever green is worn,
Are changed, changed utterly:
A terrible beauty is born.   80

1. Give a brief account of the historical event to which the speaker is referring. How does he conceive of his own relationship to this event? (How is this conception influenced by his being Irish?) How, in precise terms, have things been "changed utterly" by the event? Does the speaker assume that his audience's perception of themselves and history will have been "changed utterly" as well?

2. What is the thematic relationship between the first and last stanzas of the poem? (Analysis of structure is here necessary to your elucidation of thematic meaning: try not simply to account for the shift from a "private" to a "public" perspective, but to explain the symbolic relationship between them.) How does the line *I write it out in a verse* focus this relationship?

3. What do the following phrases suggest about the thematic meaning of the poem: *a terrible beauty; the casual comedy; enchanted to a stone; a shadow of cloud on the stream / Changes minute by minute; can make a stone of the heart*? How does the image of the

stone in the stream focus this image (see lines 41–64)? How does the idea of *crossing* the stream relate to the speaker's situation before and after the historical event he describes? To what extent does the speaker come to identify historical with moral awareness?

WALLACE STEVENS

THE IDEA OF ORDER AT KEY WEST

She sang beyond the genius of the sea.
The water never formed to mind or voice,
Like a body wholly body, fluttering
Its empty sleeves; and yet its mimic motion
Made constant cry, caused constantly a cry,   5
That was not ours although we understood,
Inhuman, of the veritable ocean.

The sea was not a mask. No more was she.
The song and water were not medleyed sound
Even if what she sang was what she heard,   10
Since what she sang was uttered word by word.
It may be that in all her phrases stirred
The grinding water and the gasping wind;
But it was she and not the sea we heard.

For she was the maker of the song she sang.   15
The ever-hooded, tragic-gestured sea
Was merely a place by which she walked to sing.
Whose spirit is this? we said, because we knew
It was the spirit that we sought and knew
That we should ask this often as she sang.   20

If it was only the dark voice of the sea
That rose, or even colored by many waves;
If it was only the outer voice of the sky
And cloud, of the sunken coral water-walled,
However clear, it would have been deep air,   25
The heaving speech of air, a summer sound
Repeated in a summer without end
And sound alone. But it was more than that,
More even than her voice, and ours, among
The meaningless plungings of water and the wind,   30
Theatrical distances, bronze shadows heaped
On high horizons, mountainous atmospheres
Of sky and sea.

It was her voice that made
The sky acutest at its vanishing.
She measured to the hour its solitude.   35
She was the single artificer of the world
In which she sang. And when she sang, the sea,
Whatever self it had, became the self
That was her song, for she was the maker. Then we,
As we beheld her striding there alone,   40
Knew that there never was a world for her
Except the one she sang and, singing, made.

Ramon Fernandez, tell me, if you know,
Why, when the singing ended and we turned
Toward the town, tell why the glassy lights,   45
The lights in the fishing boats at anchor there,
As the night descended, tilting in the air,
Mastered the night and portioned out the sea,
Fixing emblazoned zones and fiery poles,
Arranging, deepening, enchanting night.   50

Oh! Blessed rage for order, pale Ramon,
The maker's rage to order words of the sea,
Words of the fragrant portals, dimly-starred,
And of ourselves and of our origins,
In ghostlier demarcations, keener sounds.   55

1. Is "Ramon Fernandez" the dramatic audience of the poem? (If
so, describe his relationship to the speaker. If not, identify and describe
the dramatic audience.) Explain the thematic relationship of lines 43–
55 to the rest of the poem. (Note that analysis of symbolic structure
here precedes interpretation of thematic meaning.)

2. Explain how the following are thematically related: (a) *it was
she and not the sea we heard / For she was the maker of the song she
sang*; (b) *she was the single artificer of the world / In which she sang*,
and (c) *Oh! Blessed rage for order, pale Ramon, / The maker's rage to
order words of the sea*. How does the idea of a "rage for order" exist
as a theme in the poem as a whole?

3. What do the following phrases tell us about the speaker's
perception of himself and his situation: *body wholly body; mimic motion; veritable ocean; medleyed sound; ever-hooded, tragic-gestured
sea; it was the spirit that we sought; outer voice of the sky; the heaving speech of air; meaningless plungings of water and the wind; mastered the night; fragrant portals, dimly-starred; ghostlier demarcations,
keener sounds*. In what sense may this be described as a perception *of*
perception? May we legitimately describe this as a theme?

5

NARRATIVE

So far our discussion of critical principles has concentrated mainly on short poems, so at this point we must turn to the category of literature that includes most longer works, both prose and poetry—*narrative.* Since a narrative is simply any work that contains both a storyteller and a story, this is a broad category, and it embraces many different kinds of literature: satires like *Gulliver's Travels* and *Hudibras,* epic poems like the *Iliad* and the *Aeneid* and *Paradise Lost,* allegories like the *Divine Comedy* and *The Faerie Queene,* romances like Malory's *Morte Darthur* and Tolkien's *The Lord of the Rings,* and the novel as it has existed from the days of Defoe and Fielding to the present.

When we consider narrative in this light, we are simultaneously considering the concept of literary form most widely employed in modern criticism. To understand this concept of form, we need only think back to the concept of symbolic structure discussed in Chapter 4, for in practice they are nearly synonymous. The major distinction to be drawn is this: when we speak of symbolic structure, we are normally concentrating on the thematic meaning of some individual work, as we did, for instance, with Keats's sonnet "Bright Star." When we speak of literary form, on the other hand, we are implicitly speaking of *resemblances among works*, of the shared elements of symbolic structure that allow us to identify (on a very general level) such major categories as narrative and (on a more specific level) such categories as satire, epic, and romance.

We may usefully contrast this concept of literary form with an older notion of form that ignored symbolic structure altogether. This, an attempt to separate literature into poetry, fiction, and drama, has been described as an attempt to classify literary works by the way they appeared on the printed page. The description contains a good deal of truth: although they might have nothing else in common, an eight-line lyric like William Blake's "The Sick Rose" and a long epic like Wordsworth's *The Prelude* were according to this older view simply classified as "poetry"—a classification that recalls Jeremy Bentham's definition of a poem as any work in which the lines stop short of the right-hand margin.

It was when literary critics undertook the analysis of symbolic structure in many poems, plays, and novels that this older view of form began to appear less than useful, and a quite different concept of literary form to take its place, one deriving from the mode of analysis and interpretation we have already learned. When we concentrate on similarities in symbolic structure, for instance, we are able to identify both Bunyan's *The Pilgrim's Progress* and Spenser's *The Faerie Queene* as allegories, although one is written in prose and the other in verse, and the same principle allows us not only to identify both Dryden's *MacFlecknoe* (verse) and *Gulliver's Travels* (prose) as satires, but to see that both, as containing a storyteller and a story, belong to the more general category of narrative.

Yet it was not simply through an emphasis on symbolic structure that critics arrived at this newer concept of literary form, but through a growing awareness that the critical principles we have discussed in earlier chapters are equally true for all types of literature. When critics had attempted to separate literature simply into poetry, fiction, and drama, it had sometimes been assumed that a lyric poem, for instance, required different methods of interpretation than a novel.

But the mode of literary analysis that became the basis of modern criticism was soon to demonstrate, in the words of Cleanth Brooks, "that the critic, in moving from poetry to fiction, did not need to make basic changes in his methods, in the kind of questions that he asked, or in the way he approached the work. There obviously might be great differences in scope and scale between one's treatment of a lyric and of a novel. But the differences were not radical."[1]

Let us take a moment to consider what this means when we are approaching narrative—a novel like *Tom Jones* or an epic poem like *Paradise Lost*—as literary critics. Do we still begin, for instance, with the method of close reading discussed in Chapter 1? The answer is yes, with one qualification: since narratives are very often longer works, the process of close reading may be more selective than when we are analyzing a lyric poem or a short story. We must still understand the meaning and implication of every sentence, of course, but we shall most often choose for close analysis those passages that relate to some identifiable theme, or that promise to tell us something important about symbolic structure.

We have already seen how this process works in Chapter 4, where our analysis of Pope's *Rape of the Lock* concentrated on certain passages widely separated from each other in a five-canto narrative poem, but closely related in terms of thematic meaning. Having isolated those passages, you will recall, we proceeded to give them the same kind of detailed attention as we gave to Jarrell's "Next Day" and Donne's "Love's Alchemy" in Chapter 1. The importance of close reading when dealing with narrative is demonstrated even more dramatically in the student essay appearing on pages 153–161: here, the recurrence of a single important image—exposed tendons and bone —over a hundred pages after its first appearance in *A Moveable Feast* raises the question that the writer attempts to resolve through thematic analysis.

What, then, of the theoretical concepts we have encountered in earlier chapters? Do they also apply equally to short poems and long narratives? A moment's reflection will suggest that the answer here is also yes, that the dramatic principles (speaker, audience, tone) underlying symbolic meaning in Tennyson's *Ulysses* are also present when

1. Cleanth Brooks, "The Criticism of Fiction," in *The Critical Matrix*, ed. Paul R. Sullivan (Washington, D.C.: Georgetown University Press, 1961), p. 67.

we are reading *David Copperfield* or *Huckleberry Finn*. For Huck Finn, as we hear his voice in Mark Twain's novel, is no less a speaker than Tennyson's Ulysses, and his perception of the world is no less central to our understanding of the work. Indeed, we meet here the principle we first encountered in Chapter 2, that *Huckleberry Finn* is the world—a world of violence and trickery and adventure—as it exists in the perception of its young narrator.

In previous chapters, we saw in some detail how the method of close analysis leads from a scrutiny of words and syntax to a consideration of speaker, audience, and tone, and then to interpretation of symbolic meaning. To see how the same process applies in the interpretation of narrative, let us look at the way a well-known literary critic (Walter J. Ong) goes about analyzing the opening sentences of Hemingway's *A Farewell to Arms*.[2] Here is the passage:

> In the late summer of that year we lived in a house in a village that looked across the river and the plain to the mountains. In the bed of the river there were pebbles and boulders, dry and white in the sun, and the water was clear and swiftly moving and blue in the channels.

Using only this short passage as an example, Ong is able to isolate a crucial feature of tone: " 'Across the river.' What river? The reader apparently is supposed to know. 'And the plain.' What plain? '*The* plain—remember? 'To the mountains.' What mountains? Do I have to tell you? Of course not. *The* mountains—*those* mountains we know. We have somehow been there together. Who? You, my reader, and I."

How does the writer arrive at these inferences about the relation of speaker to audience in *A Farewell to Arms*? Through the same method of analysis discussed in Chapters 1 through 4. Here the writer is directing our attention to one important feature of syntax: the recurrence of definite articles—*the* rather than *a*—throughout the passage. The crucial point here is that "the indefinite article tacitly acknowledges the existence or possibility of a number of individuals beyond the immediate range of reference," whereas "the definite article signals some previous, less definite acquaintanceship." (If I were telling you about an accident that you had not witnessed, I would say "I was hit by *a* car yesterday." But if you had been standing on the side-

2. Walter J. Ong, S.J., "The Writer's Audience Is Always a Fiction," *Publications of the Modern Language Association* (January 1975), p. 13.

walk at the time, and we were discussing the accident later, I would say "When I was hit by *the* car. . . .") This is how Hemingway's use of the definite article "signals the reader that he is from the first on familiar ground."

In *A Farewell to Arms*, therefore, we have a narrative that presents "the known world, accepted and accepting. Not presentation, but recall." The narrator in this situation "needs only to point, for what he wants to tell you about is not the scene at all but his feelings. These, too, he treats as something you really had somehow shared, though you might not have been quite aware of it at the time. He can tell you what was going on inside him and count on sympathy, for you were there. You *know*. The reader here has a well-marked role assigned him. He is a companion-in-arms, somewhat later become a confidant." Here, as close analysis of a short passage from *A Farewell to Arms* leads to a significant generalization about the nature of dramatic audience in Hemingway's novels, we see how our general method of literary analysis is employed in the interpretation of narrative.

When we are dealing with narrative, then, we are on familiar ground with regard to both theory and method, and all that is demanded of us is a certain adjustment of critical perspective: since we cannot discuss every important feature of a work as long as *Tom Jones* or *Paradise Lost*, we choose to concentrate either on some significant theme or, as in the essay on dramatic audience just quoted, on some element that illuminates the symbolic structure of the work. At the same time, there are several specialized critical concepts that are helpful when we are discussing narrative, and that derive from the nature of narrative as a literary form that tells a story. To these we may now turn.

Let us begin with the normal distinction, introduced in Chapter 2, between speaker and narrator. When we observe that every narrator of a literary work is a speaker, we are simply observing that the interpretation of narrative employs the critical techniques we have previously discussed, especially those involving analysis of the manner in which the symbolic meaning of the work derives from some speaker's perception of the world. When we observe that not every speaker is a narrator, however, we introduce a more specific consideration, for we are now focusing our attention exclusively on speakers who are storytellers. In the concept of the speaker as storyteller we encounter a new dimension of dramatic situation: we are now dealing not simply with the speaker's perception of the world, but with his perspective on the story he is telling.

One way of describing the perspective of the storyteller in narrative is to describe his *point of view,* which as an interpretive concept allows us to identify the two main types of narrator we encounter when reading narrative: the *omniscient narrator* and the *first-person narrator.* An omniscient narrator is in this terminology one who knows everything that is going on in the story, including the thoughts and feelings of the characters. The first-person narrator, on the other hand, has a more restricted view: he himself is a character in the story, and he speaks as a participant. In simple terms, therefore, point of view is a matter of whether the story is told in the first or the third person.

Yet what makes the concept of point of view so useful in the interpretation of narrative is far more complex, for the distinction between the omniscient and the first-person points of view corresponds to a distinction between two fundamentally different ways of seeing the world. To undersand why this is so, let us think for a moment about the way our world appears to us normally—that is, as we live in the moment and operate within our own horizons of space and time. Although space and time constitute, for all of us, the organizing categories or boundaries of experience, it is evident that these have little to do with "objective" space and time—space as it is measured in feet and inches, time as it is measured by clocks.

Let us concentrate for a moment, for instance, on the notion of space as a horizon of personal experience. Imagine that you and I are seated across from each other in a restaurant in Boston, you as a visitor from Los Angeles who is seeing the city for the first time, I as a native of Boston who has never been away from the eastern United States. Although Los Angeles and Boston exist, for both of us, as cities separated by an identical geographical distance, we inhabit worlds that radiate outward from different centers—in our imaginary case, you undoubtedly feel that you are far away from the center of the world as you perceive it, I that you have arrived, from a relatively distant outpost, at the center of mine. And, of course, we are both right, for we are dealing not with geography but with space—what is "farther from" and "closer to"—as it exists within two worlds with different centers and horizons of personal experience.

Within these horizons of personal experience, it is similarly evident that you and I see things in ways so different as to constitute different worlds. Given our horizons of time and space, and the differences in the worlds they bound, the mutual friend (let us call him Sam) who joins us at our table in the Boston restaurant has in effect walked into two different worlds. Here again we may appeal to the notion of space as a horizon of experience, for we remember that our friend Sam, although he is sitting in a location far from the center of your world, is simultaneously at the center of mine. Yet things are far more complicated than that, for Sam also exists in a different relation to everything in my world (which includes, among other things, you) than he does to everything in yours—he is, in a manner of speaking, two different Sams.

The concept of point of view recognizes, in literary and interpretive terms, what seem to be the two essential perspectives deriving from this notion of a perceptual world. To the first-person narrator, who speaks from within the horizons of his personal experience, the people in his world are in psychological terms opaque—he may guess, as we all guess, at things like motives and emotions, but he does so from outward appearance (just as we, seeing a friend wince, conclude that he is in pain or discomfort). The first-person narrator as it were views his world on its own level—he cannot see directly into the consciousness of other characters—and the "I" of the story represents a center of personal consciousness from which everything radiates outward.

The principle of narrative omniscience, on the other hand, gives us a perspective from which the world of the story is viewed from somewhere above its own level—not only do we see characters as people inhabiting worlds with different horizons (and we are aware of what those horizons are and how they relate to motive and action), but we enter along with the narrator into their consciousness, seeing the world as they see it even as we see them as creatures of their world. The omniscient narrator is thus a storyteller who presides over the world of the story in a manner that implies simultaneous detachment and involvement, and whose double perspective on events determines our own.

The concept of the narrator's relative detachment from or involvement in—that is, psychological participation in—the story he is telling brings us to another concept that has become central in modern interpretation of narrative: the concept of *distance* (also referred to as *aesthetic distance*). Every narrator, whether first-person or omniscient, may be viewed as operating somewhere between the two extremes of complete detachment and complete involvement, and his psychological participation in the story is an important element in its meaning.

To see how the concept of aesthetic distance is used to describe varying degrees of involvement within a story, let us briefly consider some scenes from Jane Austen's novel *Pride and Prejudice*. The heroine of the novel is Elizabeth Bennet, a brilliant and beautiful young woman surrounded by thoughtless and foolish sisters and a mother who is, in varying degrees, silly, vulgar, self-centered, and morally obtuse. The world she inhabits is the world of the English countryside in the early nineteenth century—"three or four families in a country village," as Jane Austen described her favorite subject—where a young woman's main task in life is to make a favorable match: that is, to marry a man with an estate large enough to support her in comfort. The real story of the novel begins with Elizabeth's meeting with Fitzwilliam Darcy, a man who is both highly intelligent and very wealthy, but who is at the same time insufferably proud. He scorns Elizabeth at their first meeting (at a formal dance), considering her not only physically unattractive but far beneath him in social terms, and she returns the favor, thus forming the prejudice against him (and his pride) suggested in the title.

On the level of plot, the story of *Pride and Prejudice* is thereafter the story of the series of events that brings Elizabeth and Darcy together—or rather, to the mutual realization that theirs has been from the first a marriage of true minds. On the thematic level, however, what happens is far more complicated, for as events unfold we see the world of the novel separating into two spheres: a "community of sense" at the center of which stand Elizabeth and Darcy, and a sphere of vulgarity, egocentricity, obtuseness, and general ill-breeding that contains all the characters in the story who exist beyond its invisible circumference.

When we describe the world of *Pride and Prejudice* in this manner, the concept of aesthetic distance becomes central to our sense of where the circumference of the community of sense is drawn, for it is the narrator's involvement in the emotional life of her heroine—

reflected in the greater degree of omniscience with which the heroine's thoughts and emotions are reported—that provides the moral context within which we judge the other characters. Since point of view underlies the possibilities of aesthetic distance, let us begin with a passage early in the story that reveals our narrator's point of view:

> Within a short walk of Longbourn lived a family with whom the Bennets were particularly intimate. Sir William Lucas had been formerly in trade in Meryton, where he had made a tolerable fortune and risen to the honour of knighthood by an address to the King, during his mayoralty. The distinction had perhaps been felt too strongly. It had given him a disgust to his business and to his residence in a small market town; and quitting them both, he had removed with his family to a house about a mile from Meryton, denominated from that period Lucas Lodge, where he could think with pleasure of his own importance, and unshackled by business, occupy himself solely in being civil to all the world. For though elated by his rank, it did not render him supercilious; on the contrary, he was all attention to everybody. By nature inoffensive, friendly and obliging, his presentation at St. James's had made him courteous.

The story is being told, it seems, from the omniscient or third-person point of view, although there is nothing in this passage to suggest that the narrator sees directly into Sir William's consciousness—indeed, her description of Sir William is one that might be given by any neighbor with some psychological penetration and a good-humored sense of proportion. Yet it is evident that some sort of moral judgement is being made here, and that Sir William is, however inoffensive, something of a fool. If, during his term as mayor, the King. had never visited his small town, he would undoubtedly be today what he then was, a moderately successful provincial tradesman. The King did visit, however, and Sir William was called upon as mayor to give the welcoming speech, and was rewarded (as was then customary and wholly routine) with a knighthood. To be knighted meant making a single journey to the court at St. James—where the King would be knighting perhaps twenty other mayors who had made welcoming speeches in other small towns—and this has become the central event of Sir William's life—"the distinction," the narrator tells us with quiet irony, "had perhaps been felt too strongly."

5. NARRATIVE

To feel the distinction too strongly means, in Sir William's case, to believe that the addition of a routinely bestowed title to his name, a title moreover earned by giving a thoroughly routine welcoming address on the dusty main street of a small provincial town, has made him a higher sort of being. His "disgust to his business and to his residence" when he returns from St. James is a naive form of self-deception—he is still, of course, only a provincial tradesman, although he now sees himself, after one brief visit, as a polished, sophisticated creature of the court—which, however innocent, is also a form of blind egocentricity or vanity. In a world where foolishness and vanity banish characters to the sphere that lies outside the community of sense, Sir William is obviously going to earn just such banishment.

If the narrator of *Pride and Prejudice* is omniscient, however, why does she not, instead of giving us an indirect and external estimate of Sir William, simply tell us what has gone on in his mind? This is a question of aesthetic distance, for the narrator's indirect and external description of the situation is a means of maintaining her distance from Sir William and his world, of remaining detached from his attitudes and values—it is only *within* the novel's community of sense that we discover the characters who share the narrator's values, which are the values according to which characters like Sir William are to be judged. This is why, at the other extreme, we explain in terms of distance the greater degree of omniscience with which Elizabeth Bennet's thoughts and emotions are viewed: as the heroine of the story, Elizabeth stands at the center of the community of sense, and it is through the narrator's greater psychological involvement in her emotional life that the sense of distance dissolves.

Let us consider two episodes that measure the dissolution of distance between narrator and heroine in the novel. The first, which occurs early in the story, records Elizabeth's reaction to two women whose ill-breeding consists in looking down on everyone they consider to be beneath them in wealth and social standing—"they were rather handsome, had been educated in one of the first private seminaries in town, had a fortune of twenty thousand pounds . . . and were therefore in every respect entitled to think well of themselves, and meanly of others." Elizabeth's sister Jane, always disposed to see the best in everyone, has been finding reasons why they are "very pleasing women":

Elizabeth listened in silence, but was not convinced; their behaviour at the assembly had not been calculated to please in general; and with more quickness of observation and less pliancy of temper than her sister, and with a judgment too unassailed by any attention to herself, she was very little disposed to approve them. They were in fact very fine ladies; not deficient in good humour when they were pleased, nor in the power of being agreeable where they chose it; but proud and conceited.

The second episode, which occurs much later in the story, contains Elizabeth's reaction to Darcy's first offer of marriage. The background is this: Darcy has not only admitted to Elizabeth that he has successfully plotted to keep his friend Bingley from proposing marriage to Elizabeth's lovely and sensible sister Jane, but that his reasons for doing so have caused him to struggle with himself before making his own proposal to Elizabeth. For although Jane and Elizabeth are beautiful and sensible, they would bring with them as relatives by marriage their silly sisters and their vulgar mother, and their "condition in life" is moreover inferior to that of both Bingley and himself. Here is Elizabeth's reaction:

That she should receive an offer of marriage from Mr. Darcy! that he should have been in love with her for so many months! so much in love as to wish to marry her in spite of all the objections which had made him prevent his friend's marrying her sister, and which must appear at least with equal force in his own case, was almost incredible! it was gratifying to have inspired unconsciously so strong an affection. But his pride, his abominable pride, his shameless avowal of what he had done with respect to Jane . . . soon overcame the pity which the consideration of his attachment had for the moment excited.

If, as we are reading the first of these two passages, we think back to the narrator's earlier description of Sir William Lucas, we shall immediately recognize a decrease in distance: when we are told that Elizabeth "was not convinced" by Jane's arguments, we are obviously getting a direct report on her thoughts and feelings. At the same time, we are just as obviously getting some sort of external estimate of Elizabeth and her situation: it is the narrator who tells us that Elizabeth has "more quickness of observation and less pliancy of temper than her sister," and in the moment when she makes the observation we have left the world of Elizabeth's private thoughts. If the passage describing Sir William Lucas moved us toward an extreme of detachment, this episode seems to put us somewhere in the middle distance between complete detachment and complete involvement.

Actually, what is happening in the first of our two passages is that we are encountering an alignment of values between narrator and heroine: if this is the way Elizabeth views the two "very fine ladies," it is also the way they are viewed by the narrator, and the result is an expansion and stabilization of the set of values that define the community of sense in the novel. Once this set of values and the community it defines are established, we get the complete dissolution of distance evident in our second passage, which gives us in very direct terms the world as it appears to Elizabeth in the moments after Darcy's proposal —"That she should receive an offer of marriage from Mr. Darcy! that he should have been in love with her for so many months!"

Now let us look briefly at how the varying degrees of aesthetic distance we have traced in *Pride and Prejudice* work to define what we have called the community of sense in the novel. Here what is important is that the narrator's psychological involvement in the emotional life of her heroine creates an axis of values around which the rest of the story revolves, and which determines in very precise terms which characters are to be excluded from the community of sense. Here is the narrator's account of a scene in which Elizabeth's mother, who has been working mightily and openly to marry her eldest daughter Jane to the wealthy and personable Mr. Bingley, loudly celebrates her anticipated success for the benefit of her friend Lady Lucas. The setting is a dinner party, and we begin by viewing the scene through Elizabeth's eyes:

> . . . deeply was she vexed to find that her mother was talking to that one person (Lady Lucas) freely, openly, and of nothing else but of her expectation that Jane would be soon married to Mr. Bingley.—It was an animating subject, and Mrs. Bennet seemed incapable of fatigue while enumerating the advantages of the match. His being such a charming young man, and so rich, and living but three miles from them, were the first points of self-gratulation; and then it was such a comfort to think how fond the two sisters were of Jane, and to be certain that they must desire

the connection as much as she could do. It was, moreover, such a promising thing for her younger daughters, as Jane's marrying so greatly must throw them in the way of other rich men. . . . She concluded with many good wishes that Lady Lucas might soon be equally fortunate, though evidently and triumphantly believing there was no chance of it.

To fully appreciate Mrs. Bennet's vulgarity of mind and spirit in this scene, it is of course helpful to have followed her from the beginning of the novel, but even this brief passage may indicate the forms it usually takes. There is, first of all, the consideration that Mrs. Bennet has no right to be celebrating publicly a proposal of marriage that has not taken place (in fact, Bingley leaves the neighborhood without proposing to Jane), and that, even if it had taken place, a person less ill-bred than Mrs. Bennet would not be celebrating publicly her own role as the manipulator who brought it about. Then there are all the other hints that Mrs. Bennet is less interested in her daughter's happiness than in the way the greatness of the marriage will reflect on her —"His being such a charming young man, and so rich . . ."—and in the opportunities it will afford her to work, in just as open and ill-bred a manner, for the marriages of her younger daughters, "as Jane's marrying so greatly must throw them in the way of other rich men."

All this would be tasteless enough even if it arose from Mrs. Bennet's genuine satisfaction at Jane's approaching happiness, but what it really is, as the narrator tells us, is "self-gratulation"—an impossibly vulgar woman's trumpeting of what she takes to be her own good fortune. It is almost too much to bear when Mrs. Bennet adds shameless arrogance and hypocrisy to her list of sins against social decency, using the occasion to remind Lady Lucas that her own daughters stand little chance of making marriages this good: "she concluded with many good wishes that Lady Lucas might soon be equally fortunate, though evidently and triumphantly believing there was no chance of it." It is almost too much to bear, at any rate, for Elizabeth, who has been forced to listen to the whole thing from her end of the table:

> In vain did Elizabeth endeavour to check the rapidity of her mother's words, or persuade her to describe her felicity in a less audible whisper; for to her inexpressible vexation, she could per-

ceive that the chief of it was overheard by Mr. Darcy, who sat opposite to them. Her mother only scolded her for being nonsensical.

"What is Mr. Darcy to me, pray, that I should be afraid of him? I am sure we owe him no such particular civility as to be obliged to say nothing *he* may not like to hear."

"For heaven's sake, madam, speak lower.—What advantage can it be to you to offend Mr. Darcy?—You will never recommend yourself to his friend by so doing."

Nothing that she could say, however, had any influence. Her mother would talk of her views in the same intelligible tone. Elizabeth blushed and blushed again with shame and vexation. She could not help frequently glancing her eye at Mr. Darcy, though every glance convinced her of what she dreaded; for though he was not always looking at her mother, she was convinced that his attention was invariably fixed by her. The expression of his face changed gradually from indignant contempt to a composed and steady gravity.

Mrs. Bennet's behavior in this scene alone, obviously, is enough to banish her forever from the novel's community of sense, but what concerns us here is the sense in which the banishment is an effect of point of view and aesthetic distance. In the first of the two passages above we have the familiar alignment of point of view between narrator and heroine: although we know, since the narrator is describing the scene, that we are dealing with her point of view, her omniscience in recording Elizabeth's emotions puts us, in terms of distance, inside the heroine's consciousness: "deeply was she vexed to find that her mother was talking to that one person," etc. We view the scene, therefore, as it is viewed *both* by narrator and heroine.

Yet what is significant about this alignment of point of view between narrator and heroine, or—to put it another way—the dissolution of distance between them, is that it places Mrs. Bennet on the other side of an invisible barrier she does not suspect to exist. Elizabeth's vexation, and the implied moral disapproval on the narrator's part as she describes the scene, belong to a world of refined sensibility—of tact, delicacy, consideration for others—to which Mrs. Bennet is quite simply oblivious: it is not that she is ignoring or flouting the conventions of this world, for she is too silly and too vulgar even to be aware that they exist. If Mrs. Bennet is to be excluded from the novel's community of sense, therefore, it is in large part because she cannot conceive of its very existence.

The greater degree of omniscience in the next passage contains the same implications, but now the focus expands to include the reaction of Darcy as registered, in the throes of her "inexpressible vexation," by Elizabeth. The effect is to include Darcy, again in terms of point of view and distance, in the community of sense, for the intensity of Elizabeth's embarrassment can only be explained by her awareness that Darcy's indignant contempt springs from the same source as her own shame, and that this source is a sensibility closely resembling her own. Long before Darcy has declared his love for Elizabeth, therefore—and perhaps before he even realizes that he is in love with her—we begin to understand why, despite all the real and apparent obstacles to their union, they are destined for each other.

This is the manner in which the concepts of point of view and distance allow us to account in very precise terms for the way the narrator's perspective on the story determines its major themes. At times, the problems that arise may be extraordinarily complex, but the concepts themselves are simple enough, and are extremely useful when we are writing about narrative.

The other two terms that come up most often when we are dealing with narrative are *character* and *plot*. If you have ever written a critical essay on a novel or a short story, you have already had to deal with the problem of character in narrative; since it is a popular topic, you may even have done a paper on "The Character of Heathcliff in *Wuthering Heights*" or some such subject. It might be useful to begin by asking exactly what we mean when we talk about "character" in this sense.

The concept of character in narrative begins with the presence in the story of other people besides the narrator. Of all the observations we can make about the narrator's relation to these characters, the most important one seems to be that they are autonomous—that is, they have minds and wills of their own, and they are capable of independent action. This is a complex consideration, because it means that in a very special sense a character in a story or a narrative poem exists simultaneously inside and outside the narrator's field of perception.

That sounds like a paradox, but it is only a way of accounting for the autonomous role of fictional characters. In any story, of course, we are continuously dealing with the narrator's perception of a given character, but at the same time there is something the narrator cannot account for, simply because nobody ever can: the character's power to act independently in any situation in which he finds himself. As a storyteller, the narrator is in the position you and I are in when we observe the actions of other people: he can describe and analyze, interpret motives and feelings, even—according to the conventions of fiction—tell us what is going on in somebody's mind, but the one thing he cannot do is to tell us what a character will do next. (As we shall see in a moment, the possibility of plot arises from the presence of autonomous characters in the story.)

This returns us to a familiar principle, for as an autonomous figure a character in a story is himself a speaker who adjusts to the presence of his dramatic audience, and who reveals his conception of himself and the world as he speaks. In this sense, the problem of character in narrative involves the concept of tone we discussed in Chapter 4, only this time in a slightly more complicated context: in a story, we are dealing with the attitude a character reveals not just in a single dramatic situation, but in successive dramatic situations, and we are looking for the conception of self that accounts for his shifts in tone.

When we deal with the problem of character, we are really trying to define the sense in which people in stories, even as they behave differently in successive situations, remain the same. We can see why variations in tone are so important here: they are our key to the motives and attitudes which underlie actions. You may recall, in Mark Twain's *Huckleberry Finn*, the Duke and the King, two scoundrels who fall in with Huck during his journey down the Mississippi. They begin by trying to dupe each other, but soon arrive at a series of schemes to swindle other people out of their money; their crowning scheme is to pretend that they are the heirs of a rich man who has recently died. Here is the scene in which they come into possession of the money:

> They pawed the yaller-boys, and sifted them through their fingers and let them jingle down on the floor; and the king says:
> "It ain't no use talkin'; bein' brothers to a rich dead man and representatives of furrin heirs that's got left is the line for you and me, Bilge. Thish yer comes of trust'n to Providence. It's the best

way, in the long run. I've tried 'em all, and ther' ain't no better way."

Now here is the scene, a little later, where the King has been inviting the friends of the deceased to his "funeral orgies." The Duke manages to slip him a note correcting his pronunciaion (*"Obsequies*, you old fool") and he goes on:

> "I say orgies, not because it's the common term, because it ain't—obsequies bein' the common term—but because orgies is the right one. Obsequies ain't used in England no more now—it's gone out. We say orgies now in England. Orgies is better, because it means the thing you're after more exact. It's a word that's made up out'n the Greek *orgo*, outside, open, abroad; and the Hebrew *jeesum*, to plant, cover up; hence in*ter*. So you see, funeral orgies is an open er public funeral.

If we were writing about this scene, we would probably want to point out how the King's speech here defines both his character and that of his audience—the comic tension is obviously between his language, which is that of a grossly uneducated American, and his absurd pretensions to classical learning, which are part of his pose as an educated Englishman. But to an audience of country people, who have no idea of how an educated Englishman *should* sound, the pose is plausible enough, and it is apparent that the King has hit upon exactly the right tone for his purposes.

To deal with the problem of the King's character, we have to deal with the way the tone shifts between his first speech (to the Duke) and his second (to the relatives and friends of the dead man). To explain this change, we have to take into account the full implications of the King's character as a rogue—the degree to which he is self-deceived even as he tries to deceive others, for instance, or the hypocrisy he indulges, out of sheer habit, even when he is alone with the Duke—and try to show how his behavior in every situation relates to his basic idea of himself. In this case, the self-conception that explains the King's behavior seems clear—he sees himself as a successful knave in a world of fools—and our interpretation would probably focus on the ironic tension between what he is and what he thinks he is. Is he a genuinely evil figure, with his schemes for defrauding helpless people, or is he only a cheap and transparent swindler who is too inept to be dangerous? And what does his character tell us about the world of *Huckleberry Finn* as a whole?

Whenever we talk about the problem of character, we begin by attempting to explain the underlying motives that run through episodes involving a certain figure, and end with questions about their meaning in the story as a whole. At this point we are led to ask about the relation of motives to actions, which soon brings us to the concept of plot. In an important sense, plot in narrative is a function of character—that is, people act because of certain characteristic motives, and their actions influence other people who then act in another characteristic way, and so on. This is what Henry James had in mind when he asked "what is character but the determination of incident? What is incident but the illustration of character?".

The concept of plot, however, involves more than incidents determined by character, for we can divide the episodes that constitute the plot of any given narrative into two categories. The first *does* depend on the relation of character to incident, and concerns the way people unconsciously choose their own fates by acting from certain motives. The second kind of episode that occurs in narrative is a result of chance or fortune—e.g., an important character in the story dies in an accident at a crucial point in the action, or an impoverished young woman suddenly inherits a lot of money from a relative she never knew existed. In this case, plot deals with a kind of fate that isn't determined by character, and with an aspect of human existence that is beyond the control of the individual.

When we are discussing plot in narrative, we are most often concerned with the interplay of these two concepts of fate: the kind people determine for themselves through their own conscious or unconscious motives and the kind that is determined for them by the external laws of chance or fortune. Within this context, another principle often determines the symbolic meaning of the story being told: the principle of causality, or the cause-and-effect relationship existing among events in the story. The notion of causality, when it is most pronounced, gives us plot in its most "visible" form—what we have in mind when we say that an espionage thriller or a mystery story has "a good plot."

Causality is a purely abstract narrative principle, however, and one that operates differently in different narrative contexts. When we discuss plot in the comic stories of P. G. Wodehouse, for instance, we are talking about a world in which key events always seem to lead—through a perfect and hilariously logical causal process—to unforeseen results. In the novels of George Eliot, plot represents a vision of moral causality, and events are the outward manifestation of inward motivations. In *Paradise Lost*, where the great question of fate and free will is at the heart of the story, plot reflects what is called divine preordination—the story of the world as it is known, and has always been known, to God.

When the role of causality is less pronounced, we may feel more comfortable talking about the *action* of the story. This term exists as an alternative to "plot" in cases where something other than cause-and-effect is needed to explain the relationship of events within the narrative. In *The Unfortunate Traveller*, an Elizabethan narrative of the sort described as picaresque, it is the very absence of normal causality—the narrator-hero lives randomly from one day to the next —that encourages our use of the term. In *Robinson Crusoe*, the apparent plotlessness we describe by the term action is the plotlessness of everyday life as reflected in autobiographical narrative. In James Joyce's *Ulysses*, we speak of action rather than plot not because all sense of causality is absent, but because events have been so absorbed into the minds of the characters that causality is no longer of primary importance.

The concepts of plot and action represent analogous ways of dealing with the total range of events that make up a story, and in discussing them we are concerned with the role of such forces as fate, chance, choice, and causality within the total symbolic world of a given narrative—that is, we are discussing special aspects of what we have previously identified as symbolic structure. In the same way, the other terms appropriate to the interpretation of narrative represent specialized versions of concepts we have met with before: analysis of character is similar to analysis of speaker or narrator, and distance— the relation of a storyteller to the story—is only a useful way of talking about what we earlier called the speaker's relation to the world. To say that the interpretation of narrative involves no really new techniques is only to observe that literature, from short lyric poems to long novels, may be viewed as a whole.

6

DRAMA

When we turn from narrative to drama, from epics like *The Prelude* and novels like *Vanity Fair* to plays like *Hamlet* and *The Way of the World* and *Murder in the Cathedral*, we again encounter a principle we met in turning from lyric to narrative: the principle that literature, in all its variety of forms, may be seen as a whole—or, in T. S. Eliot's more elegant phrase, that literature has a simultaneous existence and composes a simultaneous order. The principle is worth restating now not only because it is a central axiom of modern criticism, but because it allows us to begin with an essential question about the relationship between drama and the forms of literature we have already discussed.

Suppose, for instance, that we chose simply to discuss drama in light of what we have learned about such forms as lyric and narrative. Then we should adopt the view, widely accepted in criticism, that "a drama is a story without a storyteller; in it characters act out directly what Aristotle called an 'imitation' of such action as we find in life.

6. DRAMA

A lyric, like a drama, is a direct presentation, in which a single actor, the poet or his surrogate, sings, or muses, or speaks for us to overhear. Add a second speaker, as Robert Frost does in 'The Death of the Hired Man,' and we move towards drama."[1] Yet this view, though extremely useful once we have seen how to interpret symbolic meaning in plays as well as in poems and novels, assumes that we have already made a certain adjustment of critical perspective.

In considering such forms as lyric and narrative, we were at every point considering not speaker or narrator merely, but speaker or narrator *in relation to* some sort of world—the twentieth-century suburban world of supermarkets and housewives in Jarrell's "Next Day," for instance, or the eighteenth-century world of beaux and ladies in Pope's *Rape of the Lock.* In lyrics or dramatic monologues, where we encounter a reality created by the utterance of a single speaker, our sense of this world is nearly inseparable from the speaker's perception of it. What might be called the primary situation in every literary work is beautifully captured in Wallace Stevens's "The Idea of Order at Key West," where the speaker, strolling at night along the shore and hearing a girl singing about the sea, realizes that song and sea belong to different spheres of reality:

> The song and water were not medleyed sound
> Even if what she sang is what she heard,
> Since what she sang was uttered word by word.
> It may be that in all her phrases stirred
> The grinding water and the gasping wind;
> But it was she and not the sea we heard.

For the word *song* in Stevens's poem we may substitute some phrase such as "image of reality." In literature, reality is always something uttered word by word, and we have seen that words in this situation always imply the presence of speaker and audience. Here we discover one reason why modern criticism assumes an essential continuity of method in moving from lyric to drama, for the methods we earlier employed to analyze the attitudes of speaker in relation to audience were developed to deal with *any* literary speaker, from the single speaker of "Love's Alchemy" to dramatic characters like King

1. Robert Scholes and Robert Kellogg, *The Nature of Narrative* (New York: Oxford University Press, 1966), p. 4.

Lear or Lady Macbeth. This is why, for instance, the interpretation of drama follows the steps already familiar to us, beginning with analytic reading and moving systematically toward thematic interpretation, for every line in a play—like every line in a poem, every sentence in a novel—gives us a world as perceived by some speaker in relation to some audience.

At the same time, we have seen that our interpretation of every literary work must simultaneously account for certain elements of reality unperceived by the speaker, a "world" that in a sense exists outside his perception—even when, as in certain lyric poems discussed earlier, he is gazing directly at it. In narrative, where the motives and actions of autonomous characters produce the configuration of events we call plot, we encountered the phenomenon of a story that exists apart from the storyteller. This is why, in discussing the concept of distance in narrative, we found it necessary to account not only for the narrator's perception of the world but for his relation to the story he was telling. Whenever we use such terms as "plot" or "action" or "story" to describe a world of motive and action existing independent of the narrator, we are close to the conventions that govern drama as a literary form.

At just this point, we encounter the other major reason why modern criticism assumes a continuity of method in moving from poems to novels to plays, for if we use the same general method to analyze speaker and audience both in Tennyson's "Ulysses" and one of Hamlet's soliloquies, we are on equally familiar ground when we deal with the concept of plot or story in both narrative and drama. This is why, for instance, we so often come across dramatic situations in narrative. Consider the following exchange between two characters in Richard Stark's novel *Point Blank*:

> Mr. Carter permitted himself a wintry smile. "His grudge, therefore," he said, "is perfectly understandable."
> "It was him or me, Mr. Carter."
> "Of course. Is Mrs. Parker still with you?"
> "No, sir. We broke up about three months ago. I heard he killed her yesterday."
> "Killed her? Do you suppose he found out first where to find you?"
> "She didn't know, Mr. Carter."

"You're sure of that?"
"Yes, sir."

In considering such passages, we find ourselves poised on an invisible line separating narrative from drama. If we are emphasizing narrative movement, we shall probably concentrate on the first sentence: "Mr. Carter permitted himself a wintry smile." This is Mr. Carter as perceived by the narrator, and it is through the narrator's description that we gauge Mr. Carter's character and motives—we note, for instance, that a man who "permits himself" a smile is not the sort of outgoing soul who smiles readily, and that there is something ominous in the notion of a "wintry" smile. Even the simple phrase "he said" reminds us that the narrator is listening to this exchange along with us, and that when the story resumes we shall once again be looking at the world through his perspective.

Yet the exchange that follows belongs to a world that exists apart from the narrator, and obeys the conventions of dramatic presentation. All we have to do is remove the quotation marks and supply the speaker's name before each line—

Carter. Killed her? Do you suppose he found out where to find you?
Resnick. She didn't know, Mr. Carter.

—and we have the elements of a dramatic scene. Now our general method of analysis is used to discover the outlines of the dramatic situation, as when we notice that the deference paid by the second speaker to the first—"No, sir," "Yes, sir"—signals a conversation between an underling and his superior, or observe in the difference between the formal rotundity of Mr. Carter ("His grudge, therefore, is perfectly understandable") and the simple colloquiality of the underling ("It was him or me, Mr. Carter") a difference in education, social class, and, ultimately, power.

What, then, is the relation between lyric and narrative and drama? As a literary form, narrative stands at a kind of midpoint between lyric and drama, giving us (as in lyric) a single speaker whose perception of the world is our primary concern, but also (as in drama) a story that represents a world of motive and action existing apart from the speaker. In lyric and drama we thus have two extreme or "pure" possibilities of literary form, lyric portraying a situation in which the world has in a sense been absorbed into the mind of the speaker, drama a situation in which the words of two or more speakers constitute what is called the world of the play. Yet in both cases our primary sense of speaker in relation to some sort of world is central to our understanding of symbolic meaning, and to our interpretation of the work.

When we approach a play like *Hamlet* or *Arms and the Man* as an imaginary world of motive and action, we are thus able to perceive its essential resemblance to other literary forms. To borrow Cassirer's phrase once again, a play, like a novel or a poem, represents "a self-contained cosmos with its own center of gravity," and our object as literary critics is to discover and show where that center of gravity lies. In drama, however, where we encounter a world as created in the words of two or more speakers, the critical methods we have learned allow us not only to interpret separate soliloquies and speeches, but the way these relate to each other within the total context of the work. This allows us to make that adjustment of critical perspective earlier suggested by the description of a drama as a story without a storyteller.

In interpreting symbolic meaning in drama, we deal not with a world existing in the consciousness of a single speaker, but a world *as it exists simultaneously* in the minds of all the speakers in the play. This is why discussions of theme in drama so often consider some pattern of symbolic meaning as revealed in the speeches of several different characters: in any Shakespeare play, for instance, the words uttered separately by a king and by some minor character—a servant, a soldier, a gatekeeper—will reveal different perspectives on the same reality, pointing to the existence of a world that is perceived somewhat differently by rulers and peasants, but that is common to both. This is what we call the world of the play.

The interpretation of drama thus involves a mode of analysis that employs our general method to elucidate the meaning of a play viewed as a self-contained world of motive and action. To see more precisely how our general method of analysis and interpretation operates in this context, let us consider a scene in Henrik Ibsen's *A Doll's House*, a play about the disintegration of a middle-class marriage. This is the scene where Nora, the heroine of the play, suddenly perceives that her marriage to the lawyer Torvald Helmer has been outwardly happy only because she has been willing to play a subservient and demeaning role. She has never, says Nora, been really happy in marriage:

> *Helmer.* Not—not happy!
>
> *Nora.* No, only lighthearted. And you've always been so kind to me. But our home's been nothing but a playpen. I've been your doll-wife here, just as at home I was Papa's doll-child. And in turn the children have been my dolls. I thought it was fun when you played with me, just as they thought it fun when I played with them. That's been our marriage, Torvald.

On the most obvious level, *A Doll's House* is about the kind of relationship Nora describes here. At the beginning of the play, she is her husband's "songbird," his "squirrel"—a tame and somewhat flighty creature who sees herself as mentally inferior to her successful husband and wholly dependent on him. At the end of the play, when Nora announces her intention of abandoning her husband and children and going away to live her own life, she has emerged as the stronger person: the relationship symbolized by the metaphor of the doll's house has been obliterated, and with it the entire notion of women's inferiority to men. If we concentrate on the symbolic implications of Nora's words throughout this scene, therefore, we shall find ourselves focusing on the problem of women's spiritual survival in a society controlled by men:

> *Nora.* Yes, it's true now, Torvald. When I lived at home with Papa, he told me all his opinions, so I had the same ones too; or if they were different I hid them, since he wouldn't have cared for that. He used to call me his doll-child, and he played with me the way I played with my dolls. Then I came into your house—
>
> *Helmer.* How can you speak of our marriage like that?
>
> *Nora.* I mean, then I went from Papa's hands into yours. You arranged everything to your own taste, and so I got the same taste as you—or pretended to; I can't remember. I guess a little of both, first one, then the other. Now when I look back, it seems as if I'd lived here like a beggar—just from hand to mouth. I've lived by doing tricks for you, Torvald. But that's the way you wanted it. It's a great sin what you and Papa did to me. You're to blame that nothing's become of me.

When we employ our general method of analysis to elucidate this scene, we find ourselves dealing with Nora almost as if she were the solitary speaker of a poem or a story, for what is central here is Nora's own perception of herself as a doll, a toy with human form but no inner human reality, a plaything to be manipulated and set aside at will. To explain the symbolic meaning of what Nora says, therefore, we invoke the familiar coordinates of speaker, audience, and tone—in this scene, Nora in relation to her husband Torvald—and seek to discover how Nora's metaphoric description of herself as a doll-child, a doll-wife living in a doll house, relates to her total perception of herself and the world.

To this point, we are on ground familiar to us from previous chapters, and the metaphor of the doll's house allows us to isolate a central theme of the play. Yet the world of A *Doll's House* is also a world existing simultaneously in the minds of the characters who surround Nora in the story, and to explain the symbolic structure of the play we must explain their separate perceptions of the same reality. We might observe, for instance, that Nora's image of herself as a doll implies more than a notion of women as victims in a society controlled by men, for what she is describing is on a more abstract level a psychology of victimization, a way of thinking transmitted from generation to generation. She has, says Nora, been her father's doll, her husband's doll, and "the children have been my dolls."

When we turn our attention from Nora to other characters in the play, then, we may look for some related version of this idea—the same phenomenon perceived in other terms by speakers in other situations. Here, for instance, is an exchange between Nora and a family friend named Doctor Rank, a young physician doomed to an early death by his father's sexual infidelities. The venereal disease brought home by his father infected Rank as a child in the womb, and in Rank's bitter reference to his own case we have another image of victimization as something imposed by one generation on another:

> *Nora.* No, today you're completely unreasonable. And I wanted you so much to be in a really good humor.
> *Rank.* With death up my sleeve? And then to suffer in this way for somebody else's sins. Is there any justice in that? And in every single family, in some way or another, this inevitable retribution of nature goes on—

An interpretation of thematic meaning in A *Doll's House* might begin with the theme suggested here: both Nora and Rank are victims of an evil transmitted from generation to generation, and Rank's physical disease is the counterpart of the spiritual disease that, until she is brought by personal crisis to understand its nature, has afflicted Nora. Yet a simple parallel between the situations of two dramatic characters does not in itself allow us to make this sort of connection—it is because Nora and Rank both *perceive* themselves as victims, and because the way they perceive themselves is revealed in the words they speak, that our usual mode of analysis brings to light an important element in the symbolic structure of the play.

As it exists in the minds of at least two of its characters, then, the world of A *Doll's House* is one in which social institutions like marriage and family perpetuate some sort of evil, where both men and women may be the victims of social injustice, and where "society" is to be blamed for its own greatest ills. As a full analysis of the play would show, this is true for two other major characters in the story: Krogstad, a lawyer who has never managed to live down the disgrace of being involved in a forgery case, and Mrs. Linde, a widow who as a girl married for money to be able to support her mother and younger brothers. In Krogstad's disgrace, especially in relation to his small children, and in Mrs. Linde's loveless marriage we have further elaborations of the theme of social victimization.

Yet we have said that a drama portrays a world as it exists in the consciousness of all its characters, and we have so far ignored the one major character in A *Doll's House* whose perception of the world does not seem to fit the symbolic pattern we have isolated. Nora's husband Torvald Helmer, a lawyer whose upright moral character and devotion to hard work have recently led to his appointment as manager of an important bank, conceives of himself not as a victim but as a respectable representative of society and its norms—invincibly bourgeois, morally complacent, conventional to the last degree, Helmer appears in the play as a very spokesman for a society that, seen from another perspective, is the blind oppressor of its victims.

How, then, are we to relate Helmer's conception of himself and the world to that of such characters as Nora and Rank and Krogstad? Since it is the same world seen from a different perspective, our usual mode of thematic analysis leads us to look for moments in the play where Helmer refers to the same things of which we have heard Nora and Rank speak—marriage, family, the transmission of social evil from generation to generation. And when we do this, certain of Helmer's apparently random remarks, made at various moments throughout the play, leap suddenly into focus. Here is Helmer, early in the story, chiding Nora for being careless with money:

> *Helmer.* You're an odd little one. Exactly the way your father was. You're never at a loss for scraping up money; but the moment you have it, it runs right out through your fingers; you never know what you've done with it. Well, one takes you as you are. It's deep in your blood. Yes, these things are hereditary, Nora.

Here, in another scene, is Helmer's self-satisfied explanation of how criminal tendencies are passed from generation to generation:

> *Helmer.* Oh, I've seen it often enough as a lawyer. Almost everyone who goes bad early in life has a mother who's a chronic liar.
> *Nora.* Why just—the mother?
> *Helmer.* It's usually the mother's influence that's dominant, but the father's works in the same way, of course. Every lawyer is quite familiar with it. And still this Krogstad's been going home year in, year out, poisoning his own children with lies and pretenses; that's why I call him morally lost.

And now, at the crisis of the action, we hear Helmer reacting to the discovery that Nora has been guilty of forgery too, and that she is being blackmailed by Krogstad. Helmer's first excited impulse is to take their children out of Nora's care:

> *Helmer.* . . . . I've got to appease him somehow or other. The thing has to be hushed up at any cost. And as for you and me, it's got to seem like everything between us is just as it was—to the outside world, that is. You'll go right on living in this house, of course. But you can't be allowed to bring up the children; I don't dare trust you with them—Oh, to have to say this to someone I've loved so much! Well, that's done with. From now on happiness doesn't matter; all that matters is saving the bits and pieces, the appearance—

Such speeches give us the answer we are looking for: originating within the bounds of conventional middle-class morality, Helmer's vision of social reality offers a kind of unconscious parody of the way victims such as Nora and Rank perceive the world—he sees what they see, but with a perspective so limited by self-complacency that he entirely misses the significance of almost everything going on around him. In place of any real insight into events Helmer is thus able only to rehearse the tired truisms of an outworn social code—"Yes, these things are hereditary, Nora." This is in turn the social code that causes Helmer to think immediately of the opinion of "the outside world" when he discovers that Nora is guilty of forgery, and that causes the collapse of his own world when she announces, at the very end of the play, that she is going to leave him.

Our interpretation of *A Doll's House*, then, will attempt to show not only how such characters as Nora and Rank and Helmer perceive the world, but how their separate perceptions converge within the total image of reality we call the world of the play. Within this context, the same critical concepts that govern our interpretation of symbolic meaning in poetry and fiction play their usual role. When we consider Helmer as a character who misses the real significance of everything he sees, for instance, we once again encounter irony as a principle of symbolic structure, exactly as in Chapter 4. Let us return for a moment to the scene in which Helmer discovers that Nora is being blackmailed for forgery. We have heard part of his response—"all that matters is saving the bits and pieces, the appearance." Here is another:

> *Helmer.* Now you've wrecked all my happiness—ruined my whole future. Oh, it's awful to think of. I'm in a cheap little grafter's hands; he can do anything he wants with me, ask for anything, play with me like a puppet—and I can't breathe a word. I'll be swept down miserably into the depths on account of a feather-brained woman.

The symbolic relationship between this speech and Nora's metaphor of the doll's house is obvious: what Helmer does not see is that he is as much a victim as any other character in the play, that he is a puppet not of the blackmailer Krogstad but of his own subservience to social opinion—what he calls the "outside world"—and his own desperate need to preserve appearances. The concept of irony thus allows us to perceive the sense in which *A Doll's House* portrays an entire world in which men and women become puppets or dolls, playthings in human form manipulated by forces beyond their comprehension, simply by capitulating to the moral code of an imaginary "outside world," which is really an idea of middle-class society existing in their own minds.

Even so brief a discussion of *A Doll's House* will suggest how our usual methods of analysis are employed in the interpretation of drama. Once we have made the adjustment of critical perspective that allows us to see a play as a story without a storyteller, our general method is precisely that presented in Chapters 1 through 4, moving from analytic reading through interpretation of symbolic meaning to a focus on theme. As we have seen, the process begins with a careful analysis of speaker in relation to audience; here, for instance, is a scene in Shakespeare's *Measure for Measure* where a friar is talking to a young man who has been condemned to death:

> Be absolute for death, either death or life
> Shall thereby be the sweeter. Reason thus with life:
> If I do lose thee, I do lose a thing
> That none but fools would keep; a breath thou art,
> Servile to all the skyey influences
> That dost this habitation where thou keep'st
> Hourly afflict; merely, thou are death's fool,
> For him thou labor'st by thy flight to shun,
> And yet run'st toward him still.

If we were to write about this speech as given, we would go about it in the same manner as when we analyzed a Keats sonnet or a passage from Tennyson's "Ulysses"—that is, we would begin by analyzing speaker in relation to audience and by asking about the view of the world implicit in his words. And this is precisely what we do when we come to the speech as it occurs in *Measure for Measure*—in the first stage of analysis we treat it much as we would treat a dramatic monologue, trying to discover with as much precision as possible what it tells us about the speaker and his view of the world.

Yet there are important differences between the friar's speech as it occurs in *Measure for Measure* and the way it would appear if it stood alone as a dramatic monologue. First, there is the matter of dramatic situation: we know much more about the young man the friar is addressing than we would if we simply had to infer his presence from the speech itself, for he has appeared in the play before, and we have not only heard him speak but know exactly why he is in prison. Second, we know from the previous action that the friar is not a friar at all, but a Duke who, having pretended to say goodbye to the city he formerly ruled, has returned in disguise.

When our analysis begins to take such considerations as these into account, we are once more dealing with the play as a world existing simultaneously in the consciousness of all its characters—a story without a storyteller—and with a context in which the principles we have previously discussed appear as objective parts of the dramatic structure. Consider, for instance, the principle of irony, which we earlier defined as the difference between what a speaker sees and how he sees it; in the scene from *Measure for Measure* we've just looked at, the difference between what seems (a friar talking to a penitent) and what is (a Duke talking to one of his subjects) is something we perceive as an irony implicit in the situation itself. This is called *dramatic irony*, and is the exact counterpart in drama of the irony that in poetry and fiction derives from the manner in which a speaker or narrator views the world. Here is a scene from Shakespeare's *Henry the Fourth*, where the famous character Falstaff is describing his valiant defense against a body of attacking thieves:

> I am a rogue, if I were at half-sword with a dozen of them two hours together. I have 'scap'd by miracle. I am eight times thrust through the doublet, four through the hose; my buckler cut through and through; my sword hacked like a hand-saw: *ecce signum!* I never dealt better since I was a man: all would not do.

When he speaks these words, Falstaff is addressing Prince Hal, and readers of *Henry the Fourth* will remember the joke involved: it was not a dozen fierce rogues who attacked Falstaff, but the Prince and one other man in disguise. We also know that Falstaff didn't put up any valiant resistance—he ran off howling at the first sign of danger, and has torn his own clothes and hacked his sword to make it look as though he had been in a fight. Once again, then, our analysis of speaker in relation to audience allows us to see dramatic irony as a principle of dramatic structure, presenting what seems (Falstaff as having survived a courageous battle) and what is (Falstaff trying, unwittingly, to deceive the very man who attacked him) as alternative versions of the same reality, with the tension between them giving shape to the work as a whole.

Since in drama we have the last of the major literary forms, we may here attain something of a final perspective on method, for we have again found that a mode of analysis and interpretation that begins in analytic reading and analysis of speaker in relation to audience must soon introduce the principles of irony and tension to account for our sense of the work as a self-contained world. In lyric, this mode of interpretation allowed us to see the world as it existed in the consciousness of a single speaker; in narrative, the world both as existing in the mind of the narrator and as having an autonomous existence in the events making up the story. In drama, where we encounter a world existing simultaneously in the consciousness of every character in the play we are considering, our elucidation of symbolic meaning focuses on the manner in which separate perspectives converge on the same reality.

We have discussed the concepts of plot and character in connection with narrative. When we are dealing with them as elements of drama, all that is needed, again, is a minor adjustment of critical perspective. Characters in drama, like those in narrative, are autonomous beings whose motives lead to certain actions, and whose actions influence other characters, generating the sequence of events which makes up the plot.

In drama, however, we once again encounter a story without a storyteller, where certain possibilities of symbolic meaning exist in a more "pure" form than they do in narrative. We deal with these as a matter of course when we are doing an interpretation of a play, but two seem to deserve special mention: *dramatic contrasts* and *dramatic parallels* between characters. When we read any novel or narrative poem, we are aware of certain parallels and contrasts between characters, but in drama, where we perceive speech and action directly, they tend to stand out more clearly, and to be more obviously related to the symbolic level of the play's meaning.

If we were doing an interpretation of the character of Hotspur in *Henry the Fourth*, for instance, we would proceed in much the same way as we do when we're analyzing the character of the King in *Huckleberry Finn*, or Queequeg in Melville's *Moby Dick*. That is, we would have to account for the dimension of his personality that causes other people to see him as being bold to the point of rashness ("a hare-brained Hotspur, governed by a spleen"), and simultaneously for the high sense of personal honor that underlies his boldness:

> By heaven methinks it were an easy leap
> To pluck bright honor from the pale-fac'd moon,
> Or dive into the bottom of the deep,

> Where fathom-line could never touch the ground,
> And pluck up drowned honor by the locks.

An interpretation of Falstaff's character would proceed in the same way, seeking to explain the sense in which his cowardice and lying and minor treachery are redeemed by an innocence that makes them comic instead of vicious. But any treatment of Falstaff's complex character would have to include those scenes in which he reveals an outlook on life that, although it does not deny his fundamental innocence, is severely practical. Here, for instance, is the famous speech he makes just before going into battle:

> Well, 'tis no matter; honor pricks me on. Yea, but how if honor prick me off when I come on? how then? Can honor set to a leg? No. Or an arm? No. Or take away the grief of a wound? No. Honor hath no skill in surgery then? No. What is honor? a word. What is that word, honor? Air. A trim reckoning! Who hath it? he that died o' Wednesday. Doth he feel it? No. Doth he hear it? No. It is insensible then? Yea, to the dead.

At this point we are no longer dealing simply with Falstaff, but with a view of the world that is exactly opposed to Hotspur's (and that, you may recall, leads to exactly opposite behavior). When this sort of contrast between characters occurs in drama, it opens up a whole series of questions about the symbolic structure of the play as a whole. In this case, the initial contrast between Hotspur and Falstaff would lead us to an examination of the idea of honor in *Henry the Fourth,* one that would soon broaden to include other characters and episodes in which neither Hotspur nor Falstaff directly appears.

Dramatic parallels between characters exist in a similar way. When we observe that Falstaff appears in the play as a kind of father to Prince Hal, for instance, and compare the scene in which he pretends to be the King with the one in which the real King remonstrates with Hal for his dissolute behavior, we have begun to ask what the play says about the traditional problem of fathers and sons. Or when we observe that Hotspur and Hal, like Hamlet and Laertes in *Hamlet,* are young men who behave differently in parallel situations, we are again moving toward a broader interpretation of the symbolic action as a whole.

At this point, as in narrative, we begin to be concerned with plot.

Plot exists in drama exactly as it does in narrative, as a series of events caused either by the actions of the characters or by some force of fate that lies beyond their control. Once again, the absence of a narrator in drama makes this sequence of events stand out more sharply than in novels and narrative poems, and there are numerous special terms (climax, reversal, dénouement, etc.) that exist to help us describe its various stages, but as critics we are still concerned mainly with the interplay of the two kinds of fate we have talked about before: the kind people choose for themselves through their motives and actions, and the kind that is determined by the external laws of chance.

As we examine the plots of a number of plays, we are likely to find ourselves coming up against questions of the sort described as generic—that is, questions that concern drama as a *genre*, or distinct literary type. The problem of genre has drawn a good deal of attention in modern criticism, and one school of critical theory has argued that the concept is useless, or even misleading, when applied to literary works—are we really engaged in meaningful discussion when we argue about whether *Robinson Crusoe* should be classified as a novel? Let us see how the concept applies to drama, and specifically to dramatic plot.

We seem to be on safe enough ground when we describe drama it- as a genre distinct, say, from lyric poetry or prose fiction. Drama, we might say, is that category of literature made up of plays, and plays are works that consist exclusively of characters talking to each other or to themselves within the framework of the action. Even at so general a level, however, we are likely to meet with some troublesome problems: can we construct a definition broad enough to include everything we normally refer to as drama—from "stage drama" like *Oedipus Rex* and *King Lear* to "closet drama" like Byron's *Cain* and *Sardanapalus*—and yet to exclude other forms of literature that lack the mediating presence of a narrator (Yeats's "Dialogue of Self and Soul," for instance)?

Suppose, however, that our rough description of drama as a genre is taken to be satisfactory to our purposes. When we begin to examine works within the category we have described, we discover not only resemblances of plot and symbolic structure among works, but what seem to be two broad subcategories: *comedy* and *tragedy*. To use the terms comedy and tragedy in a discussion of drama is to introduce a second and more particular kind of generic reference: when we call *Hamlet* a tragedy, we are announcing not only that we are viewing it as a play, but as a play with a certain sort of hero and a specific type of plot (e.g., one that ends with the death or downfall of the hero).

The problem of genre is the problem of how such terms should be used in interpretation. In the history of criticism there have been two main uses of the genre concept, the prescriptive and the descriptive. The prescriptive use of the concept has remained roughly the same from ancient Greece to the undergraduate essays of today: "a tragedy is a work that fulfills requirements x, y, and z. *Hamlet* does/does not fulfill requirements x, y, and z. Therefore, *Hamlet* is/is not a genuine tragedy." We are engaged in a prescriptive form of critical argument whenever we try to show that Willy Loman, in Arthur Miller's *Death of a Salesman*, is or is not a tragic hero, whenever we discuss *Hamlet* or *King Lear* in light of Aristotle's theory of tragedy—whenever, in short, we compare a given play with some ideal notion of literary type.

The difficulty with a concept of a genre as an ideal type is that it commits us to a certain circularity of argument. Again, are we really involved in a meaningful discussion of *Hamlet* when, having drawn from Aristotle or Arthur Miller's discussions of tragedy or our own deliberations a notion of what tragedy is, we go on to ask whether *Hamlet* is a tragedy? The alternative, an inductive or descriptive use of such terms as tragedy and comedy, exists as a kind of critical short-hand in discussions not about genre itself, but about symbolic meaning. Here, when we call *Hamlet* a tragedy or *As You Like It* a comedy, we are simply implying that we perceive them as plays having what might be called a family resemblance to other plays within a broad inductive category.

What are the shared principles of symbolic structure that allow us to refer to certain plays as tragedies and others as comedies? As long as our use of such terms remains purely descriptive, the answer will always return us to such general aspects of symbolic structure as plot and character. When our notion of genre is primarily inductive, we arrive at something like Northrop Frye's illuminating description of plot structure in comedy:

> What normally happens is that a young man wants a young woman, that his desire is resisted by some opposition, usually paternal, and that near the end of the play some twist in the plot

enables the hero to have his will. In this simple pattern there are several complex elements. In the first place, the movement of comedy is usually a movement from one kind of society to another. At the beginning of the play the obstructing characters are in charge of the play's society, and the audience recognizes that they are usurpers. At the end of the play the device in the plot that brings hero and heroine together causes a new society to crystallize around the hero, and the moment when this crystallization occurs is the point of resolution in the action, the comic discovery, *anagnorisis* or *cognitio*.

Or his remarks on tragedy:

Whether the context is Greek, Christian, or undefined, tragedy seems to lead up to an epiphany of law, of that which is and must be. It can hardly be an accident that the two great developments of tragic drama, in fifth-century Athens and in seventeenth-century Europe, were contemporary with the rise of Ionian and of Renaissance science. In such a world-view nature is seen as an impersonal process which human law imitates as best it can, and this direct relation of man and natural law is in the foreground. The sense in Greek tragedy that fate is stronger than the gods really implies that the gods exist primarily to ratify the order of nature, and that if any personality, even a divine one, possesses a genuine power of veto over law, it is most unlikely that he will want to exercise it. In Christianity much the same is true of the personality of Christ in relation to the inscrutable decrees of the Father. Similarly the tragic process in Shakespeare is natural in the sense that it simply happens, whatever its cause, explanation, or relationships.[2]

Note the inductive character of Frye's remarks: "what normally happens," etc. By and large, modern criticism has chosen to employ generic terms in this broad descriptive way, and to use specific terms like comedy and tragedy as a form of shorthand notation in discussions of symbolic meaning. When our consideration of plot in *The Way of the World* leads us naturally to comparisons with the plot of *The Rivals*, therefore, it is not because both plays are more or less perfect embodiments of some ideal dramatic type called comedy, but because they resemble each other in certain important aspects of symbolic structure.

2. Northrop Frye, *Anatomy of Criticism* (Princeton, N.J.: Princeton University Press, 1957), pp. 163 and 208.

6. DRAMA

A discussion of dramatic plot or character that leads us in the direction of generic considerations, therefore, is really leading us toward a consideration of symbolic meaning on the broad scale. When we describe a play as a comedy or a tragedy, or when we use derived terms like comic and tragic to describe certain aspects of its meaning, we are in effect describing the way certain conventions (the death of the hero at the end of tragedy, the marriage of the lovers at the end of comedy) seem to keep recurring, in a manner that seems to suggest different ways of looking at life itself. At this point we are once again on familiar ground, for plays considered as imaginary worlds of motive and action present precisely the same problems in critical interpretation as poetry and fiction, and the same principle of recurrence we recognize in drama is something that organizes literature as a whole.

7

ORGANIZING AND WRITING THE ESSAY

The problem of organizing the critical essay is one that confronts everyone who ever attempts to write about literature, from the college sophomore to the professional literary critic, and various formulas have been evolved to deal with it. These formulas range from the maladroit to the elegant, and their very variety attests to the difficulty of the problem. Consider, for instance, a formula once popular in published criticism, one that depended on what might be called the "straw man principle." The logical structure of an essay written according to this formula almost always looked like this:

1. Smithers says X about *Pilgrim's Progress*, while
2. anyone can see that Y is the case, so
3. let us examine Y (my interpretation); now
4. as we can see, the Smithers school of criticism is wrong about *Pilgrim's Progress*.

Critics got away with this formula, one supposes, because it gave them a way eventually to arrive at a genuine interpretation, and interpretation was, after all what was wanted. But the weakness of the organization is evident: the real subject of the essay is introduced at (3), and Smithers has very little to do with it. Those critics hit upon the "straw man principle," obviously, because they could not discover any better way to begin a critical essay.

As any of us who has ever written a paper knows, it *is* difficult to begin. Even if we have a brilliant interpretation of *Pilgrim's Progress,* we cannot start out by saying "Watch—in this essay I shall present a brilliant interpretation of *Pilgrim's Progress.*" There are all sorts of solutions, ranging from the pedestrian announcement of purpose ("in this paper I shall attempt to prove . . .") to the desperate retreat to irrelevant but unassailable fact ("John Bunyan, the author of *Pilgrim's Progress,* was a tinker"), but most of them are unsatisfactory in one way or another. The problem of organizing our essay, obviously, is closely related to the problem of beginning it.

Let us suppose, then, that we have already chosen the subject of our paper, and that sometime in the next few hours we have to sit down and begin writing it. If the topic has been assigned ("The Character of Iago in *Othello*"), we have no problem—we know enough about character, dramatic irony, symbolic meaning, etc., to interpret Iago's role in the play, and we only have to worry about presenting our interpretation effectively. If we have only been assigned a general essay on a work, our task is a little harder: we obviously don't have the space to do a full interpretation, so we have to pick out a theme, or some problem concerning narrator or tone or audience, to write about.

We have already looked at one major theme of Pope's *Rape of the Lock,* so let's use that as an example, and pretend that our essay is going to be about "The Battle of the Sexes in *The Rape of the Lock.*" If you look back to Chapter 4, you'll see that our discussion of this theme concentrated on three different passages from the poem, and that it had a simple logical structure:

> 1. Belinda's petticoat is described as a kind of armor, which implies that she's preparing for some sort of battle; and
> 2. the card game in Canto II is described as an actual battle between Belinda and the young lord who admires her, which implies that sex is an element in their conflict; and

3. the "war" of looks and reproaches in Canto V, where the women take sides against the men, makes it clear that the idea of conflict between the sexes is a major theme of the poem.

Then, you'll recall, we made some general observations that explained the source of the theme: that there is a necessary antagonism between women who are supposed to guard their virginity and men who regard it as a challenge, that an attractive young woman, who stands to lose her independence if she gets married and her attractiveness if she delays getting married too long, is in a morally ambiguous position, that this ambiguity introduces an element of conflict into her relations with men, and so on.

That sounds like a clear enough progression of ideas, and in fact it duplicates the form of many critical essays written by students: once a writer has found a way to begin his argument, his natural tendency is perhaps to proceed from the particular to the general, from specific passages to related passages to a general conclusion. In skeleton form, such essays go like this: (1) introductory paragraphs, (2) argument, (3) major point of argument. But it is clear that this doesn't get us past the problem of how to begin the essay: if we adopt this form, we still face the dilemma of what to put in those introductory paragraphs.

For just this reason, the form is one that should *not* be adopted in writing criticism. I used it because we were taking *The Rape of the Lock* as an example in a general discussion of theme, but when writing about a specific theme in a specific work, an alternative form is much more effective:

1. major point,
2. substantiation,
3. conclusion.

It may be startling to be told that an essay should begin with its major point, instead of leading up to it carefully, but it is a fact that most critical papers, after beginning awkwardly, end where they should have begun.

We can see why this is so if we consider the difficulties of starting the usual way. It is possible simply to begin by quoting Ariel's description of Belinda's petticoat, by pointing out that the petticoat is being

139

described as armor, and by noting that armor is something used in war, but our reader, even if he sees that our analysis of the passage is correct, still doesn't have any clear idea of where we are going. When we start out with two or three paragraphs on sexual antagonism in the poem, on the other hand, and suggest that it has its source in the paradoxical position of a marriageable young woman surrounded by admirers, our readers know immediately where they are, and look forward to seeing how we are going to support our general interpretation.

If we were to arrive at these same observations at the end of our paper, they would be a formal conclusion. But by beginning with them, before we have attempted to prove anything, we make them not conclusive but suggestive—that is, they both orient our readers and awaken their interest in our argument. Now, when we introduce Ariel's description of Belinda's petticoat, we can proceed easily to show how the episode implicitly depends on an idea of conflict between the sexes, how the petticoat is symbolically a kind of armor against sexual conquest, and so on. From this point, our argument develops logically toward a full substantiation of our original generalizations.

But what do we now do for a conclusion? Simple: our conclusion returns us to the observations we made at the beginning of our essay, and allows us to treat them as proven assertions. With the full weight of our argument behind us, we are in a position to make some final statement about the wider implications of the theme we have written about—to suggest, for instance, that *The Rape of the Lock* is a poem not only about conflict between the sexes, but about the conflict that always arises when our freedom as individuals is threatened by social conventions, and about the way people attempt to compromise with society without compromising themselves. If we have begun our argument well, and if our interpretation of the work is solid and perceptive, this sort of conclusion will suggest itself naturally, and will leave our readers with the feeling that we have increased their understanding of the work.

This logical structure will serve well in any critical essay you have to write—not just the ones about theme, but about character, tone, audience, and the rest. Before going on to the matter of style, let us make a few general observations about organization, choice of topic, and related matters.

In a way, the most difficult topics to write about are the assigned ones: you may have a splendid idea about the conflict of the sexes in *The Rape of the Lock*, and feel unfairly put upon when you go to class one day and find "The Dramatic Function of Clarissa's Speech" listed on the board as the assigned topic. But you shouldn't feel too disappointed, for two reasons: (1) Clarissa's speech is part of the theme you have already chosen to write about, and (2) you can still ask your professor to allow you to write on the original topic.

Professors do not assign topics because it's fun to make them up: they do it because, if they don't, twenty students are sure to show up during office hours lamenting that they "don't know what to *write* about." When you do know how to do criticism, however, this is never a problem, and any teacher will usually be delighted to learn that you have already worked out an idea. Sometimes, however, assigned topics are necessary for other reasons. In this case, you'll find nine times out of ten that writing on the topic only involves modifying the argument you were going to develop anyway, and all you have to worry about is a change of emphasis.

Of all assigned topics, the most difficult ones are the "compare and contrast" variety—e.g., "compare the character of Clarissa in *The Rape of the Lock* with the character of Jane Bennet in *Pride and Prejudice*." The least effective way to handle this topic is the one that seems most obvious: i.e., to observe that whereas Clarissa and Jane are alike in respects A, B, and C, they are different in respects D, E, and F. That sort of thing doesn't lead to any useful conclusion, and it inhibits the development of any real critical argument.

A more effective way to approach a compare-and-contrast topic is to take a deep breath and settle down to consider our full interpretation of the two works in question. In this case, for instance, we would begin by observing that the idea of conflict between the sexes is a major theme of *Pride and Prejudice* as well as *The Rape of the Lock*. Once we realize that Clarissa and Jane Bennet both adopt conciliatory roles in this conflict, and that each stands in contrast to a more strong-minded heroine (Belinda and, in *Pride and Prejudice*, Elizabeth Bennet), we are moving toward a more general kind of inquiry: why do Clarissa and Jane appear as conciliators in two works concerned with psychological conflict between the sexes? (because they don't understand how serious the conflict is? because they're less independent than other women? because they genuinely dislike the idea of conflict altogether?) Whatever the answer, we are now getting close to the real subject of our essay. A compare-and-contrast topic is not a liability but an advantage, because it is almost always large enough to accommodate whatever argument we want to make.

Once we have chosen our topic, or been assigned one, and worked out the main line of our argument, there comes a problem in choosing the passages we shall use to support it. In a way, this is easy: there are a hundred passages in *The Rape of the Lock*, for instance, that support the argument we've been discussing. But that's precisely what makes our task, in another sense, a difficult one. Even when we are dealing with a more restricted topic, we are sure to have a dozen passages marked by the time we've finished reading a novel or play or long poem. (I suggest, by the way, that you mark lightly in the margin with a pencil: underlining ruins books for reading later on. And *never* mark a library copy: people who do that are the lowest form of humanity.)

In this situation, I have one suggsetion: use as few quotations as possible to prove your case, and make sure that your readers are always aware that they are following a general and coherent argument, not a plodding discussion of particular passages. The dullest kind of critical essay is one that simply labors along from quotation to quotation, offering disconnected insights along the way. You can avoid writing that kind of congested essay by restricting the number of long quotations (the kind that are set off from the text) you allow yourself—there should be no more than three long quotations in a ten-page paper—and by incorporating important words and phrases from other crucial passages into your own discussion.

If I were writing our essay on *The Rape of the Lock*, for instance, I wouldn't bother to quote the entire passage describing Belinda's petticoat: it is just as easy to make the same point in a sentence that incorporates the crucial phrase—"In describing Belinda's petticoat as 'a sevenfold fence,' Ariel is metaphorically comparing it to the armor of an epic hero." Whenever a critic quotes a long passage and then proceeds to quote most of its important words and phrases in the commentary that immediately follows, he did not need to quote it in the first place.

Finally, a related point: there is no need to quote passages in the order they occur in the work. Sometimes one has to, but in general it is a sign of a badly organized essay: if we have thought our argument through, we have chosen certain passages because of their relevance to that argument, and there is no reason to let the order of their occurrence in the work organize our argument for us. One good way to avoid this is to type the passages on separate cards, and to experiment with different sequences until you discover the one that makes your point most effectively.

As this is an introduction to the theory and methods of literary criticism, and not a guide to prose composition, our consideration of style will necessarily be brief. Yet the importance of style in literary criticism cannot be overemphasized, for until critics find an alternative way of expressing insights about literary meaning—an unlikely event, on the face of it—literary criticism is going to continue to be written in language, and anything written in language introduces considerations of style.

There is perhaps nothing so easy to talk about, and so difficult to make good sense about, as prose style. For making sense in this context would seem to involve translating the elements of good style into clear principles that can be understood by any beginning writer. That may well be an impossible task—not because those principles don't exist, but because they are so inseparable from good style itself that they resist abstraction and neat tabulation. The relationship between good style and the "principles" of good style seems inevitably to raise the question asked in Yeats's "Among School Children": "how can we know the dancer from the dance?"

At the same time, it is possible to talk sensibly about *approaches* to good style—that is, about the conditions under which good style is most likely to occur if it is to occur at all. My own views in this matter closely parallel those of Richard A. Lanham, whose *Style: An Anti-Textbook* has so brilliantly suggested an entirely new program for the teaching of college composition: "a course in writing has no immediate context—it is not writing *for* anything—and it has no *subject.* What do you write *about?* Until prose style concerns everyone, and not just English departments, the first question can find only incomplete answers. Students will remain flaccid and unmotivated until some connection is made between writing and the motives their culture really honors. Perhaps the best way to ensure 'A' papers would be to pay a cash reward. Until we attain that golden sequel, surely what is called for is a theory of prose composition which stresses its pleasures as well as its duties, and supplies some kind of context for these pleasures."[1]

Although the fact is seldom appreciated by students struggling through their mandatory freshman-year composition course, writing well—discovering exactly which words and sentences perfectly express a complex idea—*is* a pleasure. Yet the freedom of expression that a competent prose style allows is something difficult to earn and even more difficult to retain. In a context where the only real answers lie in the classroom and immediately beyond—that is, in constant writing under the supervision of a talented teacher—we shall perhaps do best to restrict ourselves to a few important general observations.

Let us begin with an observation central to the whole business of good writing: in any situation where we are concerned with the relation of style to language, style *is* meaning. All of us have a natural tendency to think of "ideas" as things that exist apart from the words that express them—we talk about "saying the same thing in different words"—but a moment's reflection will show us that this is an unlikely state of affairs, something like supposing that a statue could exist apart from the marble out of which it was created, or that a human face could exist apart from its features. John Henry Newman put it this way: "thought and meaning are inseparable from each other. Matter and expression are parts of one: style is a thinking out into language." We can no more separate style and meaning, says Newman, than we can separate light and illumination, or the convex and concave of a curve.

The consequences of this, when we are approaching style as something to be practised and learned, are very important: whenever we "say something in different words," we have said a different thing.

1. Richard A. Lanham, *Style: An Anti-Textbook* (New Haven, Conn.: Yale University Press, 1974), p. 13.

Here is what happens when George Orwell puts a passage from the King James Bible into "different words":

> Here is a well-known verse from *Ecclesiastes*:
> "I returned and saw under the sun, that the race is not to the swift, nor the battle to the strong, neither yet bread to the wise, nor yet riches to men of understanding, nor yet favour to men of skill; but time and chance happeneth to them all."
> Here it is in modern English:
> "Objective consideration of contemporary phenomena compels the conclusion that success or failure in competitive activities exhibits no tendency to be commensurate with innate capacity, but that a considerable element of the unpredictable must invariably be taken into account."

This is of course a parody of "modern English"—the passage occurs in Orwell's well-known essay "Politics and the English Language"—but it suggests something every writer is compelled sooner or later to take seriously: since style is inseparable from meaning, what is called "bad style" is really a question of bad meaning.

Any approach to good style, then, is simultaneously an approach to effective and original thinking. "The great secret how to write well," said Alexander Pope, "is to know thoroughly what one writes about, and not to be affected . . . to write naturally." We shall consider the second part of Pope's precept in a moment; let us here consider the first. Writing an essay in literary criticism is in one respect no different from writing an essay in subjects like history and philosophy and even science: although every subject has a vocabulary distinctly suited to its area of inquiry, the process of good writing begins with having a sound and clearly developed central idea.

When we are writing a critical essay, then, our immediate concern is with the interpretive point we shall be trying to make about the symbolic meaning of some poem or play or novel. To "know thoroughly what one writes about" is, in this context, to make an intelligent use of the critical techniques we have earlier discussed in detail, and to be certain, before we begin to write, that we really do have an original point to make. This is a less elementary consideration than it sounds: simply *seeing* a pattern of symbolic meaning in a literary work is exciting, and every writer has had the experience of being enticed into writing before he knows exactly what he is going to say.

One solution to the problem of style, therefore, is suggested by the organizational strategy outlined earlier, or something very like it: when we consciously set out to begin an essay with our major point, it is at least certain that our argument *has* a major point. A useful way of verifying this is to try writing the major point of the argument in a few sentences before beginning the actual essay. (Let us assume we have isolated the symbolic pattern we wish to discuss, have chosen the passages we shall use to support our argument, etc.)

Let us return, for the last time, to our imaginary essay on *The Rape of the Lock*, and consider the sense in which our concern for organization is also a concern for style. We have isolated the theme of sexual antagonism, and we have chosen our passages from the poem —the dressing scene, the card game, etc.—and now we try to state the argument of our essay in a sentence or two. If, after a due amount of thinking, the sentence we come up with is something like "the battle of the sexes is an important theme in Pope's *Rape of the Lock*," we know that our wisest course is to make another cup of coffee and settle down to do some more thinking. If, on the other hand, our sentence reads "the theme of sexual antagonism in *The Rape of the Lock* derives from a radical ambiguity in the relations between men and women in the poem," we know we may allow ourselves to begin writing. We do know what we are going to write about, and the style of our essay will show it.

At this point, it is what might be called the purely practical aspects of style that concern us, for it is evident that our essay will not be well written if we have made mistakes in grammar, or if we have used words incorrectly. Let us consider the use of individual words: the errors we are trying to avoid on this level fall into one of two large categories—mistakes in *denotation* and mistakes in *connotation*. Any mistake in denotation is, roughly speaking, a violation of dictionary meaning. Consider the following sentences:

> Though Dorothea does not perceive it, Causaubon is merely a dull and *pedagogic* scholar.
> The indecisive Hamlet is always seen in contrast to Fortinbras, an active and *reactionary* leader of men.

Ennervated by Bingley's return, Jane quickly recovers her health and spirits.

In each case, the writer has mistaken the denotational meaning of the italicized word, and a check against the appropriate entry in any good dictionary reveals the error. (In most cases, we can guess why the error occurred: it was probably the similarity of sound between "pedagogic" and "pedantic," for instance, that led the writer of the first sentence astray.) Denotational mistakes, though every writer perhaps makes them from time to time, are among the easiest to avoid: whenever we are the least bit uncertain about the denotation of a word we want to use, the dictionary will confirm or deny our choice.

Connotation, which is the associative meaning of words, is something much more difficult to deal with, and in the last analysis seems to depend on having what is sometimes called an ear for language. Yet all of us, as speakers, and writers of English, have this to some degree, and it is something that can be developed. Consider the following sentences:

Although Wickham appears to have an attractive and *pleasurable* personality, he is fundamentally selfish and immoral.

After this discovery, the already *festering* marriage of Lydgate and Rosamond is in even deeper trouble.

The unhappiness of Imlac and his sister is *reinvigorated* by the belief that they will never escape the Happy Valley.

Throughout the story, Daisy's *profound* gaiety is in contrast to the morose thoughtfulness of Winterbourne.

In such cases as these, the dictionary is likely to be of little help, for the associative meaning of words is difficult to capture in a dictionary definition. We may discover, for instance, that *pleasurable* means "capable of affording pleasure," but that does not tell us that the word is normally used to describe some kind of experience ("a pleasurable voyage") but almost never to describe people or objects ("a pleasurable chair"). In the same way, the adjective *festering*, though it may be defined as "in a state of progressive deterioration," has a connotative meaning associated with physical corruption and decay ("a festering wound"). In the last two sentences, it is the associative meaning of the italicized words that produces a clash: we do not think of "unhappiness" as something that can be *reinvigorated*, and "gaiety" is not the sort of mood we usually describe as *profound*.

An awareness of connotative meaning is something gained primarily through extensive reading (it is also something that may be considerably refined through intelligent literary study). This is because the associative meaning of words derives from an elusive set of contextual rules underlying our normal use of language, and these rules appear to be too complex and various to be easily systematized (a practised foreign speaker of English, for instance, unless he has achieved perfect fluency, will most often make his errors in the subtle area of connotation). For those of us concerned with avoiding connotative error in our own writing, there are perhaps two main approaches: systematic elimination of errors as they occur, and avoidance of problematic words and phrases.

The best situation in which to eliminate systematically connotative errors in one's writing is the composition course, where the teacher is in a position not simply to point out that they *are* errors, but to show through examples how the same words are properly used: the associative meaning of a word like *festering*, for instance, is best made clear through a series of examples like "festering wound," "the festering condition of our slums," etc. Avoidance of problematic words and phrases, on the other hand, is a course open to a writer in any situation: although we all have our own problem words, connotative error most often results from a desire to be ornate or impressive. In such cases, choosing a simple word—e.g. *pleasant* rather than *pleasurable*—decreases the chance of error substantially.

On the next level of style, where we combine words into sentences, our major concern is with syntax. Elementary syntactic errors are simply errors in grammar: subjects that do not agree with verbs, clauses that do not go with other clauses, etc. On a more advanced plane, syntactic problems are of the sort that lead to loose sentence structure, awkwardness, and confusion about meaning. Consider the following:

1. In writing the *Canterbury Tales*, Chaucer's irony was directed at all levels of society.
2. "Ode to Autumn" is a poem by John Keats. It is about nature. It is also about man's response to nature.
3. The eighteenth-century notion of society, appearing in the

novels of the time, shows that novelists of the eighteenth century for the most part tended to concentrate on the comic side of the people and situations with which they were concerned to portray.

The first sentence above may be taken to illustrate the category of syntactic error that consists of simple grammatical mistakes: sentence (1) may look acceptable if we read it quickly, and we in any case have a good idea of what the writer means to say, but a closer inspection reveals the breakdown in syntax—read slowly and carefully, the sentence implies that "Chaucer's irony"—not Chaucer himself—wrote the *Canterbury Tales*. This is a variety of grammatical error that is discussed in detail in basic composition guides (our first sentence represents a class of sentences like "While walking down the street, the light turned red"), and it is by far the easiest to avoid: a simple observance of the rules of correct grammar taught in junior high and high school prevents such mistakes.

At a slightly higher level, however, syntactic error appears no longer as error—there may be nothing *grammatically* wrong with a syntactically awkward sentence—but as a matter of style. It is at this point that we begin to be concerned with the second part of Pope's precept: another great secret how to write well, we recall, is "not to be affected . . . to write naturally." As prose composition has been taught in America for many years, this notion of naturalness has been interpreted as being synonymous with such qualities as brevity and clarity. There is much to be said for these as stylistic principles, so long as we realize that they simply indicate one possible style among many.

Consider, for instance, the second and third sentences in our collection. Sentence (2) illustrates a kind of style that has been pushed *too* far in the direction of brevity and clarity, almost as if the writer were determined to avoid errors in syntax by writing so simply that the chances of grammatical error are reduced to an absolute minimum. Yet a perceptive essay in literary criticism is at some point going to have to deal with complex ideas, and since style is meaning in such a context, a well-written essay will have to adopt a more complex style. In this case, the sentence might be written as

Keats's "Ode to Autumn" is both about nature and about man's response to nature.

The risks of syntactic error are slightly increased here, it is true, but there has been a considerable gain in fluency.

Our third sentence, on the other hand, represents an opposite sort of problem: here, we might guess, the awkwardness reflects the writer's imperfect grasp of a number of related ideas. Under the pressure of several complex ideas, the grammar of such a sentence is all too likely to break down. We note, for instance, the two alternatives suggested by the phrase *with which they were most concerned to portray*, which may be broken up into two perfectly grammatical phrases (*with which they were most concerned, which they were concerned to portray*). The repetition of key terms—e.g., *eighteenth-century, of the eighteenth century*—also suggests that a multiplicity of ideas lies behind the awkward phrasing. If we were to rewrite such a sentence in the interests of clarity and brevity, we might simply choose to sacrifice some of the complexity suggested in the original version. This would give us a revised sentence something like

> Eighteenth-century novelists for the most part tended to concentrate on the comic aspects of human experience.

If, on the other hand, we want to preserve the complexity of implication that we suspect lies behind the original syntax, we must first isolate the ideas involved. We shall have to guess at the writer's intended meaning, but the ideas are perhaps as follows: (1) eighteenth-century novelists for the most part tended to write about contemporary society, and (2) they also chose to concentrate on the comic aspects of human experience. Our rewritten version of the sentence will thus read something like this:

> Eighteenth-century novelists, in choosing contemporary society
> as their subject, chose also to concentrate on the comic aspects of
> human experience.

The elimination of syntactic awkwardness is not always as simple as placing a subordinate idea in a subordinate clause, but the process usually does begin with isolating the separate ideas that seem to be jostling each other for space within an awkwardly constructed sentence. We are now in a position to see why such syntactic problems as awkwardness and even ungrammaticality are really problems in meaning: to discover that one idea is subordinate to another, and that the grammatical resources of our language allow for the perfect expression of delicate distinctions, is once again to discover that style and meaning are the same.

As we have observed, the notion that good prose style is always a style exemplifying clarity and brevity has recently met with serious challenges (most persuasively in Lanham's *Style: An Anti-Textbook,* from which we have already quoted). There is in any case little question that this prescriptive notion of good style is severely limited— are we to call such writers as Sir Thomas Browne, Samuel Johnson, and Henry James "bad stylists" because they fail to meet its demands? —and that the whole problem of teaching and learning prose style is in the process of being reconsidered. Our present concern with the style of critical essays should be viewed against the background of this larger reconsideration.

As critics, we must also remain aware of the distinction between learning literary criticism and learning how to write effective prose. The critical concepts and techniques we have discussed will allow us to undertake an intelligent interpretation of poems and novels and plays, but writing good prose involves a quite different set of techniques. These are best learned in the classroom, for writing demands constant guidance and supervision: in a famous psychological experiment, blindfolded subjects were asked repeatedly to throw darts at a dartboard, but were not told at any point how they were doing. To no one's surprise, their accuracy did not improve in the least. This may be taken as a kind of parable of learning prose style—if its moral were more persuasively advanced, one suspects that the college composition course, now so often regarded as an unpleasant obstacle, would be among the most popular electives.

WRITING AND REVISION

The two versions of the critical essay that follow were written in response to a specific assignment in a freshman seminar. The first part of the assignment was to write a short critical essay on Hemingway's *A Moveable Feast,* isolating a theme that would illuminate the work as a whole. Then, after essays had been read and intensively analyzed in class, students were asked to write a revised and expanded version of their original paper.

The class had, during the first month of the course, been introduced to the critical concepts discussed in our earlier chapters, and had written four previous essays. The aim of this assignment was to encourage thoughtful revision of style and organization, and to suggest strategies for expanding a single critical insight into an essay that would deal with its broader implications. This writer chose to expand his original essay by relating the theme of luck to the theme of discipline in *A Moveable Feast*.

In connection with the principles we have discussed in this chapter, what follows may be taken as "before" and "after" versions of a single essay: note that the organization of the essay changes significantly between the first and second versions, and that the second version demonstrates, especially, the benefits of careful stylistic revision. At the same time, the second version reveals a good practical grasp of the critical concepts discussed in Chapters 1 through 4.

Luck in A Moveable Feast

Luck develops as an important theme throughout Hemingway's A Moveable Feast. It is closely linked with many of the activities and events of the book, with young Hemingway's writing success, with gambling on horses and playing poker in the mountains, with the happiness that Hemingway and his wife share. Symbols of luck appear several times in the narrative: knocking on wood to preserve luck, the rabbit's foot and horse chestnut in his right pocket. Even the language suggests that the narrator is viewing things from a perspective of luck. Hemingway writes of "betting on our life and work."[1] and later of "the terrible odds" against Fitzgerald (176).

Luck comes to represent those qualities which set the young Hemingway apart--his youth, his happiness, his artistic ability. The early usage of the word "luck" in the story establishes the identification of luck with those characteristics. The first time it is used, Hemingway savors the luck which enables him to write successfully (12). The next time, Hemingway and his wife think how lucky they are after delightedly contemplating all the wonderful things they are going to do in the rest of the day (37-38). The narrator confirms the generality with which luck is to be conceived in the passage when Hemingway and his wife return from a successful time at the racetrack. Young Hemingway comments on how lucky they were, but observes that they did of course have good information and advice. Hadley replies that he is being too literal, that she conceives of luck in a much broader sense. The words which the narrator uses to describe Hemingway's statement-- "simple," "stupid"--convey clearly that he wants the reader to share Hadley's perspective (56-57).

7. ORGANIZING AND WRITING THE ESSAY

The theme of luck focuses the reader on the passing of Hemingway's youth and the loss of his happiness as the central developments of A Moveable Feast. First, the narrator employs the symbolism of luck to highlight the happiness of the time. Beyond description of the events of the period, luck provides a way of stepping back and generalizing: "in those days you did not really need anything, not even the rabbit's foot" (96). The symbols of luck again underscore the goodness of the time in the incident where a café-intruder becomes a critic:

> "Hem I have to tell you that I find your work just a little too stark."
> "Too bad," I said.
> "Hem it's too stripped, too lean."
> "Bad luck."
> "Hem too stark, too stripped, too lean, too sinewy."
> I felt the rabbit's foot in my pocket guiltily. "I'll try to fatten it up a little."
>
> (95)

Hemingway has just described how the skin of the rabbit's foot has been worn away, leaving only the bare bones and the sinews. The critic's statements take on a double meaning for they are as much an attack on Hemingway's luck, his rabbit foot, as they are a criticism of his writing. Hemingway's luck, like his happiness and youth, set him apart from the critic.

Second, in order to focus attention on the passing of that first period in Paris, the narrator uses the theme of luck to foreshadow. The past tense of the quote "in those days you did not really need anything, not even the rabbit's foot" (96) emphasizes the finiteness of the time. When young Hemingway and

154

his wife are rejoicing in how lucky they are, the narrator writes
"like a fool I did not knock on wood" (38), again making it clear
there is an end in sight.

Finally, the narrator uses the symbolism of luck to make
more vivid the conclusion of those days in Paris. In the final
winter the memory which stands out most prominently is that of a
man killed in an avalanche: "his neck worn through so that the
tendons and the bone were visible" (204). This is remarkably
suggestive of the earlier description of the rabbit's foot: "the
fur had been worn off the rabbit's foot long ago and the bones
and the sinews were polished by wear" (91). The image suggests
that just as the man could not withstand the onrushing avalanche,
Hemingway's luck, his youth, his happiness, could not oppose the
pressure of time and the people crowding in around him.

Hemingway's use of luck provides an insight into the relation
between the older Hemingway, the narrator, and the past he is
describing. Throughout the book the relation is nostalgic, but as
the book progresses there is a subtle shift. At the beginning of
the book Hemingway communicates the feeling that if only the
young Hemingway had perceived the fragility of his happiness, he
could have preserved it. In an early passage he writes, "'We're
always lucky,' I said, and like a fool I did not knock on wood.
There was wood everywhere in the apartment to knock on too'"
(38). But as the story develops the narrator gradually attains a
new perspective. By the end he writes:

"We're awfully lucky."

"We'll have to be good and hold it."

We both touched wood on the café table and the waiter came to
see what it was that we wanted. But what we wanted not he, nor

155

anyone else, nor knocking on wood or on marble, as this café table-top was, could ever bring us.

(176)

He has realized that the end of the period had to come, that it is impossible to retain one's youth forever.

1. Ernest Hemingway, <u>A Moveable Feast</u> (New York: Charles Scribner's Sons, 1965), p. 64. All parenthetical page references are to this edition.

Luck and Discipline in A Moveable Feast

Throughout A Moveable Feast, as an older Hemingway looks
back on his early years in Paris, he is simultaneously looking
back on an earlier self, a younger and more innocent Hemingway
whose innocence is finally revealed as a form of moral blindness.
The world as Hemingway perceives it at the beginning of the story
is governed by luck, a vague notion of good fortune applicable
to almost any aspect of life--a successful day of writing, the
discovery of the great Russian novelists, the happiness of early
marriage. The symbolism of luck--knocking on wood, touching a
rabbit's foot in a superstitious moment--appears at crucial moments in the story, and Hemingway's language sustains the theme,
as when he speaks of "betting on our life and work"[1] or of "the
terrible odds" against Fitzgerald (176).

Hemingway's conception of luck at this point implies an
entire conception of existence: the forces which determine the
course of one's life are ultimately beyond one's control, and
everything--even things normally supposed to be the rewards of
talent or work or self-denial--in some sense belongs to the realm
of fortune. It is good luck that Hemingway discovers the
Shakespeare and Company bookstore, "the warm, cheerful place with
a big stove in winter" where he can borrow all the books he
wants, and it is also luck that he is in love with his wife and
she with him, that he has a greater gift for writing than other
writers, that he is young and happy and in Paris.

The symbol of all this is the rabbit's foot Hemingway carries
in his pocket: "the claws scratched in the lining of your pocket
and you knew your luck was still there" (91). In the scene where
the rabbit's foot is first described--"the fur had been worn off
the rabbit's foot long ago, and the bones and the sinews were

157

polished by wear"--Hemingway is writing in a café and writing
well, but a fatuous and annoying young man intrudes:

"Hem I have to tell you that I find your work just a little
too stark."
"Too bad," I said.
"Hem, it's too stripped, too lean."
"Bad luck."
"Hem too stark, too stripped, too lean, too sinewy."
I felt the rabbit's foot in my pocket guiltily. "I'll try to
fatten it up a little."

(95)

The language used by this self-appointed critic turns a critique
of Hemingway's prose style into an attack on the rabbit's foot
and the luck it represents, the good fortune which has set
Hemingway apart from people like this, people talentless,
foolish, and hopelessly self-deceived.

A Moveable Feast is about the disintegration of those happy
days in Paris, and disintegration too may be viewed in terms of
luck or fortune. At the end of the story, when Hemingway has
begun to gain fame as a writer, a girl drawn by his fame comes to
live with him and his wife. This is the beginning of the end of
his happy marriage: "the husband has two attractive girls around
when he has finished work. One is new and strange and if he has
bad luck he gets to love them both" (210). In this context,
Hemingway's attitude towards luck represents an abdication of
moral responsibility: it is luck, not he, that is responsible.

During the final winter of the story, when Hemingway and his
wife are on what turns out to be their last skiing vacation in
the mountains, an episode occurs which seems to epitomize this
view of luck. It has been a winter of avalanches, and Hemingway

vividly remembers one in particular, and a man who did not sur-
vive: "it was a huge avalanche and it took a long time to dig
everyone out, and this man was the last to be found. He had not
been dead long and his neck was worn through so that the tendons
and the bone were visible" (204). The image, so insistently
recalling Hemingway's description of the rabbit's foot which
symbolizes his luck, suggests an unconscious connection: just as
this man was powerless to resist the onrushing avalanche,
Hemingway is powerless to resist the forces which will destroy
his happiness as a young writer in Paris.

We begin to suspect at a certain point, however, that
Hemingway's belief in luck is actually a form of self-deception.
While he has been viewing the world as governed by luck,
Hemingway has consistently chosen to live his life according to a
contrary standard--discipline. Discipline for Hemingway is a
moral principle covering every aspect of practical life: it means
trusting his own standards and writing what he knows are true
sentences before there are readers ready to accept his style, it
means submitting to poverty to devote his entire time to writing,
it means exercising all winter to strengthen his legs for the
great glacier ski runs--it means, in short, total subordination
of present satisfaction to more worthwhile future goals.

Hemingway's discipline, understood in this broad sense, is
vital to his good fortune. From this perspective, even things
normally assumed to involve pure luck become matters of discipline and work. Consider Hemingway's betting on horses, for
instance, which is so often mentioned in the story: "you watched
the prices and all the shifts of odds each time a horse you were
following would start, and you had to know how he was working and
finally get to know when the stable would try with him.... It was
hard work" (62). The same is true, most importantly, of writing:

without his constant struggle to cut out "the scrollwork of ornament," without his rising early to write before the rest of the world has awakened, without his careful resolve never to allow himself "to empty the well," Hemingway's luck in writing would vanish. Much of what he has called luck is actually the result of discipline.

In choosing to ignore all this, Hemingway forces events to an inevitable conclusion: it is not bad luck but blindness and a failure of discipline that destroys the happiness of his early days in Paris. When he becomes known as a writer, the people he refers to as "the rich" are drawn to him as surely "as birds are drawn at night to a powerful beacon" (208); he allows himself to be overwhelmed and plunges into "their fiesta concept of life" (209). He loses his discipline and, no longer trusting his own judgment of himself, turns to the rich for approval, like a "trained pig in a circus who has finally found someone who loves and appreciates him for himself alone" (209). In the same way, he does not have the discipline to put a stop to his affair with the girl who has come to stay with him and his wife: "you lie and hate it and it destroys you and every day is more dangerous, but you live day to day as in war" (210).

Once Hemingway loses his discipline, allowing the rich to overrun him, allowing the girl to remain in his home, he sets in motion the forces of bad luck he ultimately cannot resist. One thinks again of the avalanche Hemingway described earlier, which now appears in a new perspective. The victim of the avalanche was overwhelmed because he was too undisciplined to take the precautions taken by others, to start "before daylight in order not to pass the avalanche places when the sun could make them dangerous" (206). Hemingway too has begun to fail to take precautions: "I even read aloud the part of the novel that I had

rewritten which is about as low as a writer can get and much more
dangerous for him as a writer than glacier skiing unroped before
the full winter snowfall has set over the crevices" (209). And an
avalanche of misfortune overpowers him.

Only after the disintegration of his happy life in Paris does
Hemingway come to perceive the true relation of luck to discipline. He learns to recognize the destructive nature of the
parasitical world represented by the rich, and how to defend
himself from it. He comes to understand the fragility of love,
and how it must be tenderly guarded. He learns that happiness is
something that must be worked for and preserved. The nostalgia of
A Moveable Feast is a nostalgia of moral awareness, and the story
is not simply about young writers in Paris in the twenties but
about a time when life was so good that good fortune seemed only
a matter of luck.

1. Ernest Hemingway, A Moveable Feast (New York: Charles
Scribner's Sons, 1965), p. 64. All parenthetical page references
are to this edition.

8

THEORY AND PRACTICE

Critical theory is primarily concerned with the logical principles underlying the interpretation of symbolic meaning, but (like all theory) it is also concerned with logical inconsistencies—that is, with assumptions that lead us away from the interpretation of literature and into other areas of inquiry. The student who has mastered the principles of interpretation we have discussed will avoid the more common pitfalls as a matter of course, but it is perhaps worth mentioning several others that occasionally undermine the effectiveness even of experienced critics. The final three items below are in this category, and refer the reader to theoretical works in which they are discussed more fully.

The first two items, on the other hand, are practical pitfalls—two common errors in strategy that can lead astray the student who is writing, or who is in the first stages of thinking about, a critical essay:

8. THEORY AND PRACTICE

PARAPHRASE

Anyone writing a critical essay should avoid, as far as possible, saying all over again what an author has already said in the work. Suppose we are writing a paper on Wordsworth's poetry, and we have occasion to quote this passage:

> One impulse from a vernal wood
> May teach you more of man,
> Of moral evil and of good,
> Than all the sages can.
>
> Sweet is the lore which Nature brings;
> Our meddling intellect
> Mis-shapes the beauteous forms of things;—
> We murder to dissect.

There are many things we can say about this passage, but the one thing *not* to say goes like this: "in this poem Wordsworth suggests that Nature is a better source of moral knowledge than the kind of wisdom 'sages' possess. If we listen to Nature, he implies, we shall learn more about mankind than we shall from philosophy or science, because formal learning is a product of the 'meddling intellect,' which deals more with its own ideas than with real Nature, and 'mis-shapes the beauteous forms of things.'"

Everyone who has done this kind of obvious paraphrase realizes at the time that it is a substitute for genuine thought, and that it is entirely avoidable. But there is another kind of paraphrase that is harder to avoid, one that comes up when we are writing about longer works and have to keep reminding our reader of where he is: "in this scene, Cleon and Dionyza are bewailing the unhappy state of their country. A horrible famine has visited the land, and 'so sharp are hunger's teeth that man and wife / Draw lots who first shall die to lengthen life.' As they sit uttering their lament, a messenger comes with news that a fleet of ships is approaching." Sometimes this kind of thing can't be helped, but if we do it extensively our paper turns into a plot summary instead of a critical essay. As a general rule, we should try to tell our reader in as few words as possible what scene or episode we are dealing with, then get on with our argument.

READING CRITICISM

Many students, when they have a paper to write on *Adam Bede* or *Middlemarch*, give in to the temptation to run to the library and read through the shelf of George Eliot criticism, hoping to pick up some ideas. This is almost invariably counterproductive, for two reasons: (1) they should be getting their ideas from the novels, and reading criticism is an unnecessary diversion, and (2) published criticism assumes an intellectual and literary background they don't have yet, and reading it can be confusing or even misleading.

Critical books written by professional scholars represent years of work on a specialized subject (and many more years of general literary study before that), and they are really written for other scholars. This doesn't mean that students don't benefit from them. They do, but in an indirect way: their professor will have assimilated the important points, and these will be taken over in his own teaching—that is what lectures and classroom discussions are for. Teachers do have the background to read specialized criticism, and part of their job is to select and simplify, and to present major points in a way that won't be confusing.

IMPRESSIONISM

Few undergraduate critics, perhaps, are in the habit of writing things like "Shelley's style in this poem has the fragility of a rose in the waning days of summer," but it represents an extreme example of something every critic tries to avoid—making statements that apply not to the work but to his impression of the work. (This is a special version of what in critical theory is called affectivism: see "The Affective Fallacy" in Wimsatt and Beardsley's *The Verbal Icon*, cited in footnote 1 in Chapter 2.)

Certain of Shakespeare's later comedies, for instance, are commonly referred to as the "dark" comedies. As a general description, this is convenient: it simply means that Shakespeare is dealing in those plays with problems of human evil, and that they are different from the early comedies, which tend to deal with more innocent themes (usually of the boy-gets-girl variety). But "dark" is a loose metaphor, not a critical term, and it only describes someone's general impression of the plays. So if we make it a *functional* term in our interpretation

165

("In this essay I shall attempt to prove that *Measure for Measure* is a darker comedy than *Pericles*"), we are being impressionistic.

The same is true of certain words and phrases that tend to crop up even in solid, nonimpressionistic criticism. If we talk about how "robust" Browning's poetry is, or how "wispy and ephemeral" Pater's art criticism seems, or how "bleak" Nathanael West's view of the world appears, we are using impressionistic terms. In certain cases this is all right, but we must always be careful to use such terms only in the context of a controlled critical argument, so that our reader never supposes that Browning's robustness or West's bleakness is the actual subject of our essay.

AUTHOR AND WORK

One of the most important axioms of modern criticism is that we do not let biographical information about an author determine the way we read his work (or, to be more precise, the way we interpret the meaning of his work). We have already learned enough about critical theory to see why this is an error: since we are concerned as critics with the speaker or narrator inside the work, and since the speaker or narrator is never the same person as the author, it can only be misleading to confuse the two—that is, to apply something we have learned about the author to the speaker or narrator. If we assume that Jonathan Swift and Lemuel Gulliver had identical views of man and society, we are always going to misread *Gulliver's Travels*.

It is perfectly acceptable, on the other hand, to use what an author says about his work, or about any other subject, to illuminate his meaning. A good critic uses everything that might help his reader to understand his argument—a parallel passage from some work written earlier or later, a philosopher's insight into a similar problem, or even something that occurred in yesterday's newspaper. But when we use something from Wordsworth's letters to illustrate a point we are making about "The Solitary Reaper," it is exactly as though we had used a passage from *Hamlet* or Pope's "Essay on Man" to make the same point. The only time a critic uses biographical information invalidly is when he allows it to determine his interpretation—that is, when he assumes something he reads in one of Wordsworth's letters has a special authority simply because it was said by Wordsworth.

EVALUATION

In the eighteenth and nineteenth centuries, before the emergence of literary criticism as a genuine discipline, the literary critic saw himself as an arbiter of taste. Such writers undertook, presumably on the authority of their own broad literary experience, to shape the attitudes of a large reading public toward past and present literature, to tell people with only a limited amount of time for reading which works were worthwhile and which were a waste of time. This tradition of taste criticism survives today in the reviewers' columns of newspapers and magazines, where the reviewer is still sometimes called a "book critic" or a "film critic" or a "drama critic"—*critic* in this context seems to derive from *criticize*, "to find fault with"—and where the review itself is a kind of cultural consumers' report for people who want guidance on which new books to read or which plays and movies to go to.

When we write literary criticism, on the other hand, we are writing for readers whom we assume to be perfectly familiar with the work we are discussing, and who in most cases have done a good deal of thinking about it on their own. Such readers do not need to be told that a work is "good" or "bad"—that is something they can make up their own minds about, presumably—but what its meaning is. The literary critic on every level, from the student writing a critical essay to the scholar writing a book on Shakespearean tragedy, must to some extent perceive himself as a member of an intellectual community devoted to making sense out of literature as a whole.

The shift from taste criticism to modern "objective" criticism (criticism conceived of as a systematic body of knowledge about literature) took place almost imperceptibly in the earlier twentieth century: as critics became increasingly interested in the interpretation of symbolic meaning, and began to see interpretation as the main task of criticism, "taste" questions—i.e., questions of evaluation—simply began to appear irrelevant. In his *Anatomy of Criticism*, first published in 1957, Northrop Frye demonstrated at some length why they were more than irrelevant:

> Value-judgements are subjective in the sense that they can be indirectly but not directly communicated. When they are fashionable or generally accepted, they look objective, but that is all. . . .
> Shakespeare, we say, was one of a group of English dramatists

working around 1600, and also one of the great poets of the world. The first part of this is a statement of fact, the second a value-judgement so generally accepted as to pass for a statement of fact. But it is not a statement of fact. It remains a value-judgement, and not a shred of systematic criticism can ever be attached to it.[1]

The theoretical case against evaluation in criticism can be summarized as follows: since value judgements are subjective, they are in their nature unverifiable. It may appear to us, for instance, that *The Sun Also Rises* is a better novel than *Emma*, but that only means that our literary taste inclines more toward Hemingway's kind of writing than toward Jane Austen's. As soon as we try to show why one is "good" or "bad" or "better than" another, we are simply giving a disguised version of our own likes and dislikes. (We have, at the same time, abandoned the critic's task of illuminating the meaning of the work.)

From a purely logical viewpoint, that is, taste in literature may be compared to taste in clothes, or colors, or flavors of ice cream. When we are talking about books with our friends, we are perfectly justified in saying "I like *The Sun Also Rises* better than *Emma*." This is a statement that simply cannot be challenged on logical grounds. But when we make the same statement in a critical essay, we are forced to convert "I *like* X better than Y" to "X *is* better than Y." Then it is as though we had somehow undertaken to prove "logically" that chocolate is better than vanilla, or that blue is better than red.

No student writing criticism today, perhaps, has ever written an essay that incorporated value judgements in quite so crude a way ("I will now prove that X is better than Y"). But there are less obvious ways of doing the same thing, and it is well to be aware of them. If we say that *Antony and Cleopatra* is "more effective dramatically" than *Troilus and Cressida*, for instance, we are simply taking a roundabout way of describing our personal preference. The same is true when we make that kind of comparison between two parts of the same work: "Act II of *Troilus and Cressida* is more effective than Act V." Or when we talk about characters in a play or novel in a way that shows we are really making a value judgement: "Squire Alworthy is a less convincing character than Tom Jones." In addition, there are

1. Northrop Frye, *Anatomy of Criticism* (Princeton, N.J.: Princeton University Press, 1957), p. 20.

various "analytical" sounding words and phrases—"mature," "complex," "unified," etc.—that can sometimes encourage the illusion that the critic is writing about literature rather than describing his own likes and dislikes.

The question of whether evaluation has *any* legitimate place in literary criticism is a purely theoretical one, and does not much affect the way literary critics today approach literature, or even the way literature is taught in the university classroom. Some critics feel that there is an inescapable evaluative decision involved in choosing to write about one work rather than another, and many teachers feel that, in attempting to awaken their students' enthusiasm for a work or a period, they are inescapably assuming a role as arbiters of taste. But there is general agreement that evaluation is not the proper *subject* of criticism, and that the critic's major concern is with the interpretation of literary meaning.

EPILOGUE

For the student majoring in philosophy or mathematics or history, the method of interpretation taught in an introductory literature course is enough to guide a lifetime of intelligent reading, for what is really introduced in such a course is not literature but a mode of comprehension that vastly increases the rewards of reading literature. For some students, however, the introductory course is more—the entrance to advanced literary study. These remarks are addressed to those readers who intend to make English their major field of study in college.

When students choose English as a major, they are committing themselves to the systematic study of a literary tradition that extends from the earliest middle ages to the present, and their main intellectual objective—the reason for suffering through all those reading lists and papers and examinations—is to see that tradition as a whole. Up to now we have been talking about criticism as it involves the interpretation of individual works, and that is in fact where all literary study must begin. John Ciardi's remark that "poetry, finally, is one poem at a time" can be expanded to cover all of literature, for literature is, finally, one poem or play or novel at a time.

Still, although our main concern as students of literature will always be to read individual works perceptively, we cannot read seriously for very long before we begin to perceive similarities of theme and subject that raise questions about more general relationships among works. When we discussed Keats's sonnet "Bright Star" in Chapter 4, you'll remember, we discovered that it was a poem in which the speaker, as he contemplated nature in her eternal and unchanging aspect, managed to escape the natural world where seasons come and go and people grow old and die. Suppose, then, that we have finished reading "Bright Star," and before we put down our copy of Keats's poems, his "Ode to a Nightingale" catches our eye. The speaker, while listening to the nightingale's song, wishes for a magic potion:

> That I might drink, and leave the world unseen,
>   And with thee fade away into the forest dim:
> Fade away, dissolve, and quite forget
>   What thou among the leaves has never known,
> The weariness, the fever, and the fret
>   Here, when men sit and hear each other groan;
> Where palsy shakes a few, sad, last grey hairs,
>   Where youth grows pale, and spectre-thin, and dies.

Here, once again, we have a dramatic situation where a speaker enters imaginatively into a reality that exists eternally beyond the world of natural change. This time it is a nightingale and not an evening star that symbolizes unchanging nature, but the poems are similar enough to suggest several lines of inquiry. Suppose, for instance, that we decide to see how often this theme occurs in Keats; as we read, we discover that it appears again and again in his poetry, but that it is not always nature that invites the characteristic response. In "Ode on a Grecian Urn," for example, the speaker contemplates an image of human activity transformed by art into a timeless scene: "thou, silent form, dost tease us out of thought / As doth eternity . . . ." At this point, we are dealing not just with a single theme but with an imaginative world in which art and nature and human life appear as aspects of a single vision of reality—the thematic structure of Keats's poetry as a whole.

Suppose, however, that it is not the similarities between "Bright Star" and "Ode to a Nightingale" that have caught our attention, but the differences. It is easy enough to see how a star can symbolize eternal nature, but a nightingale is a bird, and we think of birds as living and dying just like people. But then we come to a stanza of the "Ode" that seems to explain things:

> Thou was not born for death, immortal Bird!
>   No hungry generations tread thee down;
> The voice I hear this passing night was heard
>   In ancient days by emperor and clown:
> Perhaps the self-same song that found a path
>   Through the sad heart of Ruth, when, sick for home,
>   She stood in tears amid the alien corn;
>   The same that oft-times hath
> Charm'd magic casements, opening on the foam
> Of perilous seas, in faery lands forlorn.

This time our inquiry seems to have led us in the direction of allusion and myth. The dramatic situation seems clear enough: while listening to the nightingale, the speaker begins to see himself as another of the innumerable listeners who have heard her song through the ages, in human history (*emperor and clown*), in sacred myth (the biblical *Ruth*), and in the imaginary world of romance (*faery lands forlorn*). Yet although we can see clearly enough how the differences between art and history and myth are dissolved here, and how the speaker has for the moment been overwhelmed by a sense of time-lessness, none of this seems to explain why he addresses the nightin-gale as *immortal bird*.

The answer lies in another myth, the Greek legend in which the lady Philomela is transformed into a nightingale and wanders eternally through the world, singing sorrowfully of the cruelty of her evil hus-band. This is the same nightingale who appears, for instance, in Matthew Arnold's poem "Philomela":

> O wanderer from a Grecian shore,
> Still, after many years, in distant lands,
> Still nourishing in thy bewildered brain
> That wild, unquenched, deep-sunken, old-world pain . . . .

The nightingale appears in English poetry almost from the beginning, and whenever we encounter her song we are almost certain to be dealing with the myth of Philomela. Keats's "Ode" is only one example among thousands of the way literature assimilates myth, and in doing so assimilates all the literature that has gone before.

Finally, let us suppose that, having read "Bright Star" and "Ode to a Nightingale," we decide to explore the idea of nature that the two poems seem to have in common. Both the sonnet and the ode are meditational poems, we observe, and in each the speaker's contemplation of nature involves a wish for immortality—if one could *swoon to death* ("Bright Star") or *cease upon the midnight with no pain* ("Ode") while lost in thoughts of eternity, it would almost be possible to become part of the natural cycle of things. When a poet invokes an idea of nature as a spiritual presence, and in contemplating her is moved to consider such things as death and immortality, we are obviously in the area of something like religious concern.

We might, once again, decide to pursue this point by looking through the rest of Keats's poetry for other examples of a "religious" view of nature, but in this case it seems more promising to ask if any other poets of his time shared a similar view. If we turn to Shelley, for instance, we find him regarding the West Wind as an *unseen presence* that governs the cycle of natural change (*wild spirit . . . moving everywhere; destroyer and preserver*), and as a source of divine inspiration:

> Be through my lips to unawakened earth
> The trumpet of a prophecy!

Or addressing a skylark much as Keats addressed the nightingale:

> Hail to thee, blithe Spirit!
> Bird thou never wert,
> That from Heaven, or near it,
> Pourest thy full heart
> In profuse strains of unpremeditated art.

As we read through other poets of Keats's time, which is of course the Romantic period, we discover that the concept of nature as a divine presence occurs again and again, not just in Shelley but in Wordsworth and Coleridge and many minor poets, and that in the literature of the period as a whole, familiar religious questions are being worked out in a new way. True, we do not find many mentions of Heaven and Hell and God, but we do find the old problems of immortality and providence and divine intelligence arising in recognizable forms, and we notice that certain words like *eternal* and *spiritual* and *prophecy* and *apocalypse* seem to occur naturally when Keats or Wordsworth or Shelley is talking about nature.

At times, in fact, we may begin to wonder if the Romantic poets are really so very far away from the old conception of a universe watched over by God and His angels, where the visible world exists only as evidence of the Divine presence. Shelley, for instance, said that he sought in what he saw "the likeness of something beyond the present and tangible object," and Wordsworth speaks in *The Prelude* about minds that, when they consider "the whole compass of the universe," are "like angels stopped upon the wing by sound / Of harmony from Heaven's remotest spheres." And consider the narrator of *The Prelude* describing a scene (he calls it a vision) of mountain and ocean and evening mist:

> There I beheld the emblem of a mind
> That feeds upon infinity, that broods
> Over the dark abyss, intent to hear
> Its voices issuing forth to silent light
> In one continuous stream . . . .

If we have read *Paradise Lost*, we shall recognize in these lines what a scholar would call a Miltonic echo. Unless we are very conscientious, there is no need to go through all of *Paradise Lost* to discover exactly which of Milton's characteristic phrases have appeared in the passage, for the important thing is that we have suddenly perceived a symbolic perspective in Wordsworth's long autobiographical poem that returns us to Milton's great epic of God and man and angels, written nearly two centuries before. At this point, other similarities between the two poems are sure to occur to us—that both belong to an epic tradition that extends back through Virgil to Homer, for instance, or that both in different ways are concerned with the same ultimate questions about man's place in the world.

This has brought us a long way from our simple inquiry about Keats's idea of nature in "Bright Star" and "Ode to a Nightingale," but any question about a literary work tends to do just that, opening up broader areas of investigation as we move from poem to poet to period, then to the literary tradition as a whole. If we wanted to explain fully the relationship between *Paradise Lost* and *The Prelude,* we would have to deal not only with English poetry from Milton to Wordsworth, but with history and philosophy and science, with Bacon and Newton and Locke and empiricism and neoclassicism and pantheism and the French Revolution. And even then, we would find ourselves looking backward from Milton to the classical writers who inspired him, or to the great issues in Christian theology that became his epic theme, and we would begin to notice that Wordsworth's view of man and nature had a profound influence on later writers, one that in certain forms has lasted to our own day. Literary history includes everything that bears on literature, early and late, and is an indispensible resource for the critic.

When students begin the English major, of course, they cannot be expected to have mastered all of Western literature, philosophy, and history—they could not do that even in a lifetime, and the most they can hope to achieve as undergraduates is some awareness of the organizing principles of literary study. But that is a significant achievement in itself, for any deep knowledge of literature is impossible until we have an intellectual map of the territory to be covered. Then, at least, we know where the blank spaces and uncharted areas are, and we can relate everything we learn to something we already know.

Eventually, when we have read most of Spenser and Shakespeare and Milton and Pope, and when names like Thomas Campion and Henry Vaughan and Matthew Prior mean something to us, we find ourselves moving more and more frequently beyond the boundaries of English literature, for the footnotes of our favorite poems and plays and novels are always referring us to Euripides or Virgil or Ovid, to the myth of Philomela or Narcissus or Sisyphus, to the biblical story of Samson or Job or Ishmael. At a certain point we no longer have to be told, but discover in a personal and intellectual sense, that English literature exists within the larger tradition of Western literature, and Western literature within the total context of what we call civilization.

Beyond this point we are on our own. Literary education aims less at the mastery of some finite body of knowledge than at the attainment of a perspective; "the critic's function," as Northrop Frye has written, "is to interpret every work of literature in the light of all the literature he knows, to keep constantly struggling to understand what literature as a whole is about."[1] It is now that we find ourselves becoming interested in the way literature relates to the larger realm of intellectual history, which contains philosophy and theology and science and art. And this is the end of our formal study of literature, whether or not we still have courses to take or examinations to pass, because from now on the only guidance we really need is our own curiosity, and our education continues for as long as we are alive to read.

1. Northrop Frye, *The Educated Imagination* (Bloomington: Indiana University Press, 1964), p. 105.

Appendix:
Some Matters of Form

As presented in the style manuals designed for professional scholars—e.g., the *MLA Style Sheet*—the rules governing footnoting, bibliographical entries, etc., are many and complex, and students sent to these sources often (and with good reason) despair of ever mastering the niceties of the *loc.*, and *op. cit.* At the same time, the simplified versions of these rules presented in the many "guides to college composition" are likely to strike students as fussy and arbitrary, largely because there is too seldom any indication of how they came to be rules in the first place.

The *MLA Style Sheet* is an admirable guide to matters of scholarly form, and there are doubtless occasions when every undergraduate critic will want to consult it on some very technical point. Yet it should be made clear that such style manuals are devised mainly to ensure uniformity and clarity in manuscripts intended for scholarly publication, and that many of their rules, especially those designed for the greater ease and comfort of editors and compositors, are simply inapplicable to undergraduate essays.

When we concentrate on everyday matters of form, the sort that are likely to occur in connection with nearly every critical essay one writes, we discover that each "rule" we encounter falls into one of two main categories, and in most cases represents a common-sense answer to some perfectly reasonable requirement. The first category, involving such matters of scholarly form as footnoting procedure, concerns the obligation of the undergraduate critic to write *as* a scholar, which here includes an obligation to provide the reader with precise references to the sources that have been consulted. Since many students unfortunately hear about these rules—especially footnote rules—in the context of dire warnings about plagiarism, their original scholarly purpose cannot be too much emphasized. In the ordinary course of things, teachers regard footnotes in student essays precisely as they regard footnotes in books or articles written by their colleagues, as a means to checking the *context* of quoted material that catches their interest.

The second category of "rules" we encounter, involving such matters as margins, spacing of quotes, etc., concerns the writer's obligation to provide a manuscript that leaves adequate space for detailed commentary, questions about inferences drawn from quoted passages, and the like. Many critical essays require only a general comment (usually given at the end), but others will raise points that call for commentary at specific points in the text: these marginal comments are, like questions raised in the classroom, a form of teaching, and observing the rules that make such teaching easier is only a matter of courtesy. (It should be added that these again conform to general scholarly practice: scholars as a matter of course ask friends and colleagues for detailed comments on their work, and are careful to obey the stylistic rules they ask their students to observe.)

Finally, we might place in this same category the rules of form which could be said to concern the writer's obligation to himself. The reasoning here is perhaps self-evident: an original and thoughtful critical essay should not look like it was thrown together in ten minutes, and an essay full of misspelled words, erratic spacing, crossings-out, writings-in, and smudged erasures cannot help giving that impression. The *minimum* requirement for any essay submitted in a college literature course is that it be neatly typed and free from errors in spelling and punctuation.

The following, which should be taken less as rules than as suggestions, may be followed in what we have called everyday matters of form.

TITLE PAGE

The normal form for the title page is

```



                  Christian Morality in
                  Barnaby Rudge




                       David A. Bachrach
                       English 98
                       27 May 1976




```

The title is centered slightly above the middle of the page. (Note that it is neither placed in quotation marks—which would indicate that it was being taken from elsewhere—nor typed in capital letters.

Putting the course title and the date of submission beneath your name is a kindness to your professor, who is sure to have on hand numerous other papers submitted in other courses and on other dates.

An alternative is to put your name, the course title, and the date of submission at the top left margin of the first page. In this case the block

David A. Bachrach
English 98
27 May 1976

should be separated by *four* spaces from the title, which is separated by *three* spaces from the body of the text.

MARGINS

The normal margin requirements call for 1½ inches at the *top* and *left* of the page, 1 inch at the bottom and right. As we have seen, these margins allow the space necessary for detailed commentary and questions, and should be regarded as a minimum requirement: when in doubt, leave more marginal space, never less.

If your typewriter has a page gauge or similar device, estimating top and bottom margins will present no difficulty. If not, you may wish to take a few extra moments to measure top and bottom margins with a ruler, putting, on as many pages as you will need for your essay, a light pencil mark at the places where you should begin and end your text. These may be erased later, and are particularly helpful in ensuring that you do not run off the bottom of the page.

INDENTATION

The normal indentation for paragraphing is 5 spaces. As we shall see, this is not arbitrary, but is related to the rule governing indentation of offset quotes.

ELLIPSIS

Ellipsis points are used to indicate that one or more words have been left out of a quoted passage.

When one or more *words* is omitted, use *three spaced* ellipsis points to indicate the omission, thus:

> I have often thought that there has rarely passed a life of which a . . . faithful narrative would not be useful.

When one or more *sentences* is omitted, use *four* ellipsis points to indicate the omission, thus:

> I have often thought that there has rarely passed a life of which a judicious and faithful narrative would not be useful. For, not only every man has in the mighty mass of the world great numbers in the same condition with himself, to whom his mistakes and miscarriages, escapes and expedients, would be of immediate and apparent use; but there is such an uniformity in the state of man, considered apart from adventitious and separable decorations and disguises, that there is scarce any possibility of good and ill, but is common to humankind. . . . We are all prompted by the same motives, all deceived by the same fallacies, all animated by hope, obstructed by danger, entangled by desire, and seduced by pleasure.
>
> Samuel Johnson, Rambler No. 60

Modern rules of form allow us to dispense with ellipsis points at the *beginning* or *end* of a quoted phrase or passage. Thus we write

> In *Rambler 60*, Johnson suggests that "a judicious and faithful narrative" of nearly any man's life would afford material for serious moral reflection.

and not

> In *Rambler 60*, Johnson suggests that ". . . a judicious and faithful narrative . . ." of nearly any man's life would afford material for serious moral reflection.

A word of caution: when omitting words, phrases, or sentences from quoted material, one must scrupulously avoid altering the meaning or emphasis of the original. This is of course true in all scholarly writing, but it is of the highest importance in literary criticism, where ellipsis can, unless perfectly disciplined, distort the meaning of a poem or passage.

BRACKETS

The principal use of brackets in critical writing is to supply parenthetical information in quoted material, where any sentence or phrase in parentheses would otherwise be assumed to be part of the original text. Thus we write

> Hazlitt says that "he [Shakespeare] had a high standard, with which he was always comparing himself, nothing short of which could satisfy his jealous ambition."

At the same time, brackets are ungainly and typographically unattractive, and should almost never be used if there is any way of avoiding them. More often than not, this can be accomplished by rephrasing, e.g.,

> Hazlitt says that Shakespeare "had a high standard, with which he was always comparing himself, nothing short of which could satisfy his jealous ambition."

QUOTATION MARKS

When a quoted phrase is part of your own sentence, quotation marks come *after* periods and commas, thus

> Hazlitt says that Shakespeare "had a high standard," and that this was related to his "jealous ambition."

Quotation marks, on the other hand, come *before* colons and semicolons, thus

> Hazlitt writes of Shakespeare's "jealous ambition": like other Romantic essayists, he assumes that one can somehow infer an author's character from his works.

When page or line numbers are cited parenthetically (more will be said on this below), the correct form is as follows:

> This is the meaning of the speaker's reference to "the everlasting universe of things" (1).

The quotation marks *precede* the parenthetical reference; commas or periods *follow* the parenthetical reference. (For some reason, students seem to have more trouble with this little rule of form than with any other.)

Single quotation marks are used to indicate words or phrases that are set off in double quotation marks in the original. Thus we quote Carlyle's sentence,

> But on the whole "genius is ever a secret to itself"; of this old truth we have, on all sides, daily evidence.

in the form

> Carlyle writes that "on the whole 'genius is ever a secret to itself'; of this old truth we have, on all sides, daily evidence."

QUOTING

Since critical essays refer more or less continuously to the work under discussion, the rules of form governing quotation are of great importance. They are few and simple, and the small effort needed to master them will be amply repaid: very often, such mastery makes the difference between an essay that reads smoothly and convincingly, and one that seems to move along in fits and starts from quotation to quotation.

At the same time, a critic who has mastered these rules comes to realize that there is an "art of quotation" that lies beyond formal systematization. Some of the strategies involved are discussed below, along with the rules of quotation.

Perhaps the most widely misunderstood rule of quotation is that governing offset quotations, the kind that are separated from the text by several spaces and indented at the left-hand margin. Most students seem to have the idea that *any* quotation over a line or two long should be offset. Thus we get frequent quotation that looks like this:

> In a curious sense, Keats's remarks about the "authenticity of the imagination" are illustrated by the account of his own state of mind given later in the same letter:
>
> > The setting sun will always set me to rights—or if a sparrow come before my window I take part in its existence and pick about the gravel.

In fact, no quoted passage is ever set off from the text unless it is of quite considerable length—*10 or more typewritten lines.* All other quotations should be run on as part of your own double-spaced text. The correct form of the above thus looks like this:

> In a curious sense, Keats's remarks about the "authenticity of the imagination" are illustrated by the account of his own state of mind given later in the same letter: "the setting sun will always set me to rights—or if a sparrow come before my window I take part in its existence and pick about the gravel."

185

(Note that the capital letter beginning Keats's sentence is put into lower case—i.e. "The setting sun . . ." becomes "the setting sun"— when the sentence is run on as part of the text. This is a minor but important rule: the first letter of a word beginning a sentence is always changed to lower case in run-on quotations. The *only* exception is words that always begin with a capital letter, e.g., John, Dartmouth College, etc.)

The rule concerning the length of offset quotations is of great importance to the appearance of a critical essay. When it is ignored, we get the sort of essay that has a continuous stream of short indented single-spaced passages meandering through a jumble of broken-up text: the result is not only unattractive, but has the effect of interrupting the smooth forward progress of the argument. When the rule is observed, the appearance is of an argument that has managed to assimilate its material gracefully: paragraphs are now coherent entities, and the occasional passage what really is long enough to justify being set off—e.g., our passage from Johnson's *Rambler* 60 on page 183—gains the emphasis its length suggests it deserves.

The rule concerning quotation of poetry is slightly different: here, any passage longer than *four* lines is set off from the text. Thus we set off a passage from George Herbert's "Jordan (I)" as follows:

> Who says that fiction only and false hair
> Become a verse? Is there in truth no beauty?
> Is all good structure in a winding stair?
> May no lines pass, except they do their duty
>   Not to a true, but to a painted chair?
>   (1–5)

The placement of the line reference here illustrates the correct form for parenthetical line or page references to *all* quotations set off from the text, either poetry or prose: the parentheses are placed just inside the right-hand margin of the offset passage. As we shall see in our section on footnoting, there is no need to use such forms as (page 6) or (p. 6), (lines 4–7) or (ll. 4–7): as the context is always obvious, page or line numbers are themselves sufficient.

When lines of poetry are run on as part of the text, as they should be with any quotation three lines or shorter, there are two alternative conventions for indicating line divisions: either may be used. The most common is the slash (virgule):

> In Herbert's "Jordan (I)" the speaker is concerned with the relationship of poetic and religious truth: "may no lines pass, except they do their duty / Not to a true, but to a painted chair?" (4–5).

The alternative, used by critics who find the virgule distracting when more than a line or so of poetry is incorporated in the text, is simply to put an extra space between the last word of one line and the first word of the next:

> In Herbert's "Jordan (I)" the speaker is concerned with the relationship of poetic and religious truth: "may no lines pass, except they do their duty Not to a true, but to a painted chair?" (4–5).

Note the form of the parenthetical reference in both cases: quotation marks first, then parentheses, then period.

The correct spacing of offset quotations is of great importance to the appearance of a critical essay. In the case both of prose and poetry, an offset passage is separated by *three* spaces at top and bottom from the double-spaced main text. An offset quote from a poem is centered on the page. To center a quote, count the number of letters, spaces, and punctuation marks in the longest line of the passage to be quoted, then divide by 2: this is the number of spaces you must backspace from the center of the page (use the paper-centering scale—the ruler-like thing on your typewriter—to find the center). When you have backspaced the proper number of times, set the Tab key in that position. Strike the Tab key twice before typing each line (remember, it is already set for a five-space paragraph indentation) and the passage will be centered.

There is a widespread misunderstanding of the rule concerning indentation of offset prose passages, and the most common practice is to treat them like poetry—that is, with a very wide margin of indentation on both left and right. In fact, a prose passage set off from the main text is indented only *three* spaces on the left—two less than for paragraph indentation—and *not at all* on the right: the right-hand margin of an offset prose passage should run even with the margin of the main text. Observance of this form, together with the rule for length of offset quotations discussed earlier, will greatly improve the appearance of any critical essay.

Finally, there is a question whether offset quotations, both poetry and prose, should be single- or double-spaced. The rule is that they should be double-spaced, exactly like the main text, but this rule is so universally disregarded that single-spacing has become the norm (probably because it comes closest to matching the printer's usual practice of using a different-sized type for offset quotations). If your typewriter has half-spacing, 1½-spacing is a perfect compromise: it leaves enough room for a teacher to note inadvertent misquoting (getting a word or punctuation mark wrong in a quoted passage, for instance) but still gives the effect of a "block" of material set off from the main text.

As we observed earlier, quotation in criticism is an art that begins where the rules of form leave off, and like all arts it is something one can learn only through practice. Yet the effects are obvious to any reader of literary criticism, from undergraduate essays to articles published in learned journals: a critic who has mastered the art of quotation gives the impression of managing the material both with authority and with perfect economy. At the other end of the scale, there are writers who never quite seem in control of their material, and whose essays seem to be little more than strings of quotations interspersed with random commentary.

In Chapter 7 we hit upon a principle central to the whole art of quotation—use as few quotations as possible to prove your case. The reason for this rule has to do with the nature of criticism, which is written for readers already perfectly familiar with the work under discussion: teachers who have assigned and lectured on *Paradise Lost* do not need to have long segments of Book I quoted for their benefit in an essay—they know the poem, and at this stage are interested in their students' insights.

A critical essay must make *some* direct reference to the text, of course—if it didn't, it would soon diffuse into vague generalities—but the rule of economy is nonetheless sound: a point that is made by quoting four lines of a poem can generally be made by quoting one, and the repeated discipline of reducing the amount of quoted material in critical writing soon sharpens one's eye for the significant single phrase or line or sentence that works as effectively as a longer passage to make the same point. The reason for quoting in a critical essay, we recall, is to show how our argument places a familiar work in a new light, and any quoted material that does not directly answer that purpose is best ruthlessly excluded.

The second version of the student essay following Chapter 7 is a good example of effective critical quoting. Note that the writer spends almost the entire first paragraph establishing the main point before introducing two simple phrases (which occur over a hundred pages apart in the book) to support the argument. Thereafter, passages quoted from *A Moveable Feast* are woven smoothly into the main argument, and the critical significance of each quote is immediately apparent. The single offset quotation—set off as much because of its dialogue form as its length—is central to the argument, and signals that the writer is about to elaborate the point so far dealt with abstractly. The result is an essay that refers continuously to the text, but where quoting is almost imperceptible and the argument always moves forward in a controlled manner.

At the same time, the essay illustrates the several strategies involved in effective and economical quotation. These may be viewed as the positive side of the negative injunction that we are not to overquote or quote needlessly, for even when we have managed to isolate the phrases and passages truly essential to our argument, there is still the matter of working them in. Let us end our consideration of quoting with an examination of three such strategies.

A major means of restricting quotation is to establish in the argument a descriptive context that makes extensive quoting unnecessary. Thus in the final sentence of the first paragraph of our sample essay the writer is able to refer to a whole range of events at the same time as he makes a point about Hemingway's language:

> The symbolism of luck—knocking on wood, touching a rabbit's foot in a superstitious moment—appears at crucial moments in the story, and Hemingway's language sustains the theme, as when he speaks of "betting on our life and work" or of the "terrible odds" against Fitzgerald.

Notice that this sentence assumes the reader's familiarity with the work: instead of quoting all or some of the passages in the work that show Hemingway knocking on wood or touching a rabbit's foot, the writer simply notes the existence and importance of such scenes— they are there, and readers may go back and check on them if they are interested.

Viewed in this light, the art of quotation is an art of making allowable assumptions, and it also says something about the sophistication of the critical point being made. As we noted in Chapter 7, writers without genuine insight into the work being discussed are especially prone to stylistic and organizational weaknesses: here, a critic whose only point was that luck *is* an important theme in *A Moveable Feast* might quote every knocking-on-wood scene available simply because he or she had nothing better to do. In the same way, the writer of our sample essay is able to make his point about Hemingway's language by quoting two phrases: the earlier part of the sentence provides a descriptive context that makes their significance immediately apparent, and they are assumed to be *representative*— behind them, presumably, lie numerous unquoted instances of similar language.

A second major strategy for incorporating quoted material smoothly is to introduce important short quotations parenthetically in sentences leading up to other quotes. An example in our essay is the sentence occurring just before the long quote on page 157:

> In the scene where the rabbit's foot is first described—"the fur had been worn off the rabbit's foot long ago, and the bones and the sinews were polished by wear"—Hemingway is writing in a café and writing well, but a fatuous and annoying young man intrudes:

Note that the short quotation set off by dashes is not there simply because the writer wants to tell us how Hemingway described the rabbit's foot—if that were the only object, the quotation would be unnecessary—but because the description is crucial to understanding both his point about the café scene and another major point made later in the essay.

Finally, a means of quotation making effective use of important short quotations (and eliminating the need for long quotations) involves sentences that preface a quoted phrase or line with a direct interpretation of its symbolic or thematic significance. Another example from our sample essay:

> In the same way, he does not have the discipline to put a stop to his affair with the girl who has come to stay with him and his wife: "you lie and hate it, and it destroys you and every day is more dangerous, but you live day to day as in war."

The words are Hemingway's, but the interpretation—that this episode represents a failure of discipline seen as a thematic concept—both refers us back to an earlier quotation and unobtrusively advances the argument.

FOOTNOTING

The rules of footnoting, so complex and forbidding as they apply to abstruse marginal situations, are in fact quite simple as they apply to ordinary critical writing, and have in any case been simplified considerably in recent years. Even the term "footnote," in fact, is retained from a time when notes were customarily placed, in space that had to be laboriously measured and marked off ahead of time, at the bottom of the page. Today, notes to critical essays are placed on a separate page at the end of the text.

The aim of all footnoting is to tell the reader, as briefly as is compatible with complete reference, the source of any material you have quoted. In literary criticism, where essays are likely to refer repeatedly to one or two works, procedure is to a very large extent governed by one major rule of reference, the rule of *parenthetical citation* we have mentioned at several points earlier in this appendix.

The basic rule of parenthetical reference is that the work from which the critic intends to quote repeatedly is given a full bibliographic reference (author, editor, place of publication, date of publication) only the *first* time it is quoted. Thereafter page numbers (or, in the case of poems, line numbers) are cited in parentheses as they occur in the text. The form both of first footnote references and subsequent parenthetical references is shown in the following sentence:

> At the very beginning of the *London Journal*, Boswell speaks of his journalizing as a means to "attending to the feelings of his heart and to his external actions,"[1] and only as the narrative proceeds do we begin to perceive another motive, equally strong, which will eventually lead Boswell to compare himself as the protagonist of his journal to "the hero of a romance or novel" (206).

If this were the first sentence of an actual essay, the slightly raised number [1] would refer us to a note at the end of the essay, the proper form of which is

1. James Boswell, *Boswell's London Journal, 1762–1763*, ed. Fred-

erick A. Pottle (New York, 1950), p. 1. All subsequent parenthetical references to the *London Journal* are to this edition.

When the reference is to a text that has been assigned to the class, most teachers encourage an even briefer form of citation:

1. John Milton, *Comus*, in *The Norton Anthology of English Literature*, pp. 1314–1338. Subsequent parenthetical line references are to this text.

In this case, the initial citation is mainly to assure your teacher that you are using a text previously agreed upon. (If you were for some reason working with an edition of *Comus* you had obtained from the library, for instance, you would provide a full citation: both the text and the line numbering might be different from the assigned text.)

In critical essays that do not draw on secondary sources, the system of parenthetical reference reduces the number of footnotes to a single citation of the text or edition used. When this is the case, the footnote may be placed at the bottom of the last page of the essay. When two or more notes occur, however, a separate page is called for: this should be headed by the word NOTES in capital letters and separated by *six* spaces from the first footnote. This page is numbered.

We have already seen the form for citation of primary texts. The order of items is

author (first name first)
title
editor (if any)
place and date of publication (in parentheses)
page or line citation

In addition, the name of the publisher should be given along with place of publication when a paperback edition *not* assigned to the class is used. The abbreviation *ed.* is used in place of "edited by." The complete form of such a note is therefore

1. Jane Austen, *Emma*, ed. Lionel Trilling (Boston: Houghton Mifflin, 1957), p. 103.

Note carefully the punctuation involved here: no comma separates the name of the editor from the parenthetical reference to place and date of publication. When the publisher's name is given, a full colon follows the place of publication. The form (p.) for (page) precedes the page reference (as is *not* the case with parenthetical page reference). Two additional features may be noted here: *every* footnote is *double-spaced*—allow *three* spaces between notes—and the first line of the note is indented *five* spaces from the left-hand margin, exactly as in the case of a sentence beginning a paragraph.

When a critical essay draws on secondary sources, two additional forms are involved. The form for citation of scholarly books is a simplified version of that for primary texts:

    3. Thomas R. Edwards, *Imaginaion and Power: A Study of Poetry on Public Themes* (New York, 1971), p. 9.

The form for citation of journal articles presents items in this order:

        author
        title of article
        name of journal
        month and year of publication
        page reference

A representative note is thus

    2. John S. Gordon, "Murphy, Mulvey, and Molly Bloom," *Joyce Studies* (Spring 1971) p. 603.

Note that the volume and number of the issue in which the article appears is not given (this is another area in which modern practice has moved toward simplification), and that quarterly journals may use "Spring," "Winter," etc., in place of the more usual month of publication.

A common scholarly practice is to abbreviate reference to well-known journals by using key letters—thus *Publications of the Modern Language Association* becomes, for footnoting purposes, *PMLA*, *Studies in Scottish Literature* becomes *SSL*, etc. A full list of the standard abbreviations is given in the annual bibliographical issue of *PMLA*; it is useful to be familiar with these abbreviations even when they are not used in footnoting, as they form part of a universal shorthand employed in literary scholarship and criticism.

These three standard footnote forms will serve for most undergraduate critical essays; a copy of the *MLA Style Sheet*—which most English departments keep in supply for undergraduate use—should perhaps be kept on hand for consultation on the rare occasions when a more complicated form of reference is in question (e.g., multi-volume works, critical articles occurring in collections, etc.).

Two final observations. In recent years, the trend has been to replace such older forms as *ibid.* and *loc. cit.* with a simple repetition of the author's name. If we have already given a full reference for Thomas Edward's *Imagination and Power*, for instance, our second reference is simply

4. Edwards, 102.

If we have previously quoted from *two* works by Edwards, the appropriate form is

4. Edwards, *Imagination and Power*, 102.

Finally, any portion of a full reference that has already appeared in the body of an essay need not be repeated in a note. If, for instance, our essay includes a sentence like this:

> In *Imagination and Power* (New York, 1971), Thomas Edwards explains that "the normal has meaning only in reference to the abnormal, the unexpected phenomenon that creates an opposing sense of mutuality where none was apparent before."[3]

our note will simply be

3. page 9.

In general, providing full or nearly full references in the body of the essay adds force to the argument: disembodied quotes from secondary sources carry less authority than those for which author and work are immediately identified. And, of course, the practice uncomplicates the business of footnoting.

STAPLES V. PAPERCLIPS

The preferred means of fastening together the pages of an essay is with paperclips; teachers almost always want to detach pages in order to write marginal comments, or to detach the page containing footnotes so that it can be read alongside the text in which quoted material occurs.

If the pages of an essay are stapled together, the staple goes in the upper-left corner of the page (the farther away from the main text the better). If proper margins are allowed, this permits the writing of marginal comments with only a minimum of inconvenience to the teacher. An essay should never be stapled together along the entire left-hand margin.

Index